How the
Stock
Markets
Work

How the
Stock
Markets
Work

A GUIDE TO THE
INTERNATIONAL
MARKETS

COLIN CHAPMAN

CENTURY
BUSINESS

First published in 1991 by Business Books Limited
An imprint of Random Century Group Limited
20 Vauxhall Bridge Road
London SW1V 2SA

Random Century Australia Pty Ltd
20 Alfred Street, Milsons Point,
Sydney, New South Wales 2061, Australia

Random Century New Zealand Ltd
18 Poland Road, Glenfield, Auckland 10, New Zealand

Random Century South Africa Pty Ltd
PO Box 337 Bergvlei 2012, South Africa

First edition 1986
Second edition 1987
Third edition 1988
Reprinted under the Century Business imprint 1992

British Library Cataloguing in Publication Data
A catalogue record for this book is available
from the British Library
ISBN 0 7126 4929 8

Set in Linotron Sabon by
Intype, London SW19 8DR

Printed and bound in Great Britain
by Mackays PLC, Chatham, Kent

Contents

Acknowledgements   viii

1   **The Global Village**   I
    The Jobber's Pitch
    The End of an Era

2   **History**   7
    Muscovy and Company
    South Sea Bubble
    Mines, Railways, Canels
    Government Debt
    The First Exchange

3   **The Footsie and the Dow**   17
    The Eurobond Market
    The Big Bang
        The Crucial Vote
        The World's First International Exchange
        The New Conglomerates
        Fast Money
    The Crash of '87
    Wall Street
    The American Prototype
    SEAQ

4   **Nomura Makes Money Make Money**   47

5   **Europe**   52
    Eastern Europe

6   **The Share Buyers**   58
    Life Assurance Companies
    Unit Trusts
    Investment Trusts

Managed Funds
The Fund of Funds
    Whitehall Relaxes the Rules
Paperchase
    The Bull Brings Taurus
Options and Futures
    Options
    Futures

7 **What About the Workers?**   85
Fabled ESOPS
Privatization: Privileges for the Workers

8 **Raising Money**   89
Going Public
Raising More Money
The Unlisted Securities Market

9 **Selling the Family Silver**   101

10 **The Takeover Trail**   105
Takeover Rules
Making an Acquisition
Growth Through Acquisition
The New Takeover Game
Where There's Junk There's Money

11 **Fast Money**   129
Investor Relations Managers
The Analysts
Financial Advisers
An Australian Invades
Battle in the Courts

12 **Policing the Markets**   141
Up Before the Courts
The New Regulators
    Disclosing Commission
    Market-rigging
The Balow Clowes Affair

13 Beyond Babel 164

Index 177

Acknowledgements

It is only three years since this book was last updated, and yet so much has changed. In London the memories of Big Bang have receded, but its impact lives on. On careful examination only the technology has improved matters. Recollections of the Great Crash of 1987 have vanished too: it is hard to believe this was the biggest fall in history. Today it seems more like a two week wonder.

As ever, the number of those who have helped is too great to be listed in full. I have benefited from the assistance of hundreds of people in London, New York, Washington, Tokyo, Frankfurt, Brussels and Sydney to put together this fourth and totally revised edition.

There are a few people who deserve special thanks: the hard-pressed reference librarians at the *Financial Times*, whose patience in dealing with my enquiries has been invaluable; Michael Hughes and the other directors of Barclays DeZoete Wedd in London, who allowed me to roam freely around their dealing rooms, John Tipper of Cazenove, who explained the arcane world of settlement, and members of staff at the London Stock Exchange. In New York Lou Dobbs and Myron Kandell of the Cable News Network were especially helpful. My editors Martin Liu and Elizabeth Hennessy made helpful suggestions and corrected glaring errors.

For historical perspective I have drawn on material culled from the archives of various stock exchanges. For those who would like to know more about the early years in London's Throgmorton Street I commend the very readable account *The Stock Exchange Story* by Alan Jenkins.

Finally my family have had to look on while an increasing proportion of our house has been taken up with books, files, documents and notes about the financial markets.

Introduction

As the world has become a global money village, so share markets have become much more accessible. From any banking hall in Britain – or by telephone from home – it is possible to buy the stocks of every major public company in the world. Science and technology has made share purchase easy. One phone call or a flick of the living room television controller will tell you what these shares are worth. At the same time, for those who wish to spread the risk, there are now funds which will invest your money in everything from environmentally-friendly green companies to recovery stocks in Thailand. And privatization has provided the opportunity for wider share ownership.

Yet I sense more people feel further away from the stock markets than ever before. In the United States and Japan – as well as in Europe – giant institutions dominate the markets, which are remote from the man in the street. To the average family the equity markets are not part of everyday life. In Britain less than 300,000 buy the *Financial Times*, while over 8.5 million read either the *Sun* or the *Daily Mirror*, both of which pay more attention to horse or dog races than to the capital markets. But even the readers of middlebrow and quality papers are often unaware of what goes on. Few know that in London there is no longer such a place as the stock market, and that dealing is all-electronic. Opinion polls show that many believe stockbrokers are disreputable. And only a small proportion of them understand that the world's sharemarkets are where the future of their savings and pensions are invested.

This book attempts to throw some light on the markets, warts and all.

1. The Global Money Village

'The real upheaval has been caused not by what has gone on in the Stock Exchange, but by the revolution in information technology. When any change or announcement is passed around the world in seconds, the old-fashioned business of trading on a floor becomes irrelevant' – Stanislas Yassukovich, one-time chairman of the Securities Association, London.

The atmosphere is like a television portrayal of the newsroom of a major newspaper, but a trifle more tense, with more fever and more bustle. Most people appear to be on the telephone, their fitful but fleeting dialogues always punctuated by taps at a keyboard, which reveal an array of coloured numbers on the bank of computer screens that dominate their desks.

Every few minutes someone gets up from his high-back swivel chair and shouts a message – or, plastic coffee beaker in hand, wanders across the floor to talk with a colleague. For the most part these dialogues are friendly and unobtrusive, but the occasional sharp-edged rejoinder reminds the observer that this is a place where serious money is at stake.

This is the equities floor of BZW, one of London's largest securities houses, where each working day tens of millions of pounds worth of shares change hands. Large stakes in major companies are bought and sold, small allotments in privatization issues are traded, money is won or lost.

Down on the floor, on the central desk, the lead salesman touches the flickering light on his telephone panel that indicates a call is waiting, picks up the phone, and rests one foot on a drawer of his desk. The caller is a fund manager from one of Britain's largest life assurance companies. He is looking to pick up a million shares in one of the big breweries.

The salesman keys into his computer the first three letters of the company's name, and the screen reveals to him that the price of the stock is higher than it has been for several weeks.

But it also shows that the posted price is only available for the purchase of 50,000 shares or less. Buying a block twenty times that size could be difficult. 'Leave it with me, we'll see what we can do, the price is good, so someone might be prepared to sell', he tells his client. After ringing off, the salesman, a man in his early thirties, shirt-sleeved and displaying wide Wall Street braces, makes a few more keystrokes. In quick succession, two graphs appear on the screen – one of them portraying the movement of the share price of the brewery group over a five year period; the other tracking it against the progress of the Financial Times Stock Exchange One Hundred Share Index, popularly known as the Footsie. The graph shows that although the shares have been rising they have been outperformed by the index.

The salesman smiles, reflecting that one of the brewery's major shareholders may well be prepared to sell, given the higher price of the stock, and the prospect that by reinvesting elsewhere there will be a more profitable return. He keys in a few more strokes, and a printer at the end of the desk produces a sheet of paper with a breakdown of the company's major shareholders, in order of size of holding. Most of the names on the list are investment institutions, life assurance companies competing with the salesman's client, pension funds, and unit trust companies. But there are also some international companies and a handful of names of wealthy individuals. The salesman calls over a junior colleague, and tells him: 'See if you can do anything with this. We need a million'.

The young man returns to his desk, picks up his telephone, and starts making calls. Within 40 minutes he is back. 'I've got them', he says, glowing with pleasure at his swift if unexpected achievement. The salesman whoops with joy, hits his client's number on the phone pad, and passes on the good news. He then walks over to another group of people sitting at another, larger bank of computers, and asks them to execute the deal. These men and women are called market-makers; they set the price for shares and, within limits, are obligated to buy and sell at the prices they set. One of them keys in both the purchase and the sale: and the deal is complete. The salesman is well pleased. His firm's commission on the transaction will be about £150,000. A small percentage of that goes towards his annual bonus.

This is the modern, high-speed, paperless stock market. At first sight it seems very different from the days prior to the City of London's Big Bang in October 1986. Then most shares were traded in a large hall known as the Stock Exchange, and the kind of transaction I have just described would have taken some weeks to complete, and could have involved several lunches or rounds of golf, as well as a considerable amount of labour. Just the task of running to earth the names of the major shareholders in the brewery group would have occupied several days.

But although in today's London share market, transactions are all electronic with the Stock Exchange floor a forlorn, forgotten and empty museum piece, there are still many similarities to the days when the large building in Throgmorton Street was alive with the thrust and bustle of scores of men and women competing to buy shares.

The Jobber's Pitch

In those days the stockbroker – or to be more accurate a dealer working for a firm of brokers – would hurry into the trading floor of the Exchange, armed with orders from clients, and make his way to one of the pitches, or stalls, specializing in the sector of the market in which he was interested. The operation was just like that of a housewife visiting a market to buy fresh vegetables. Just as the prudent shopper would check out the prices at a variety of stalls selling the same produce, so the dealer would seek quotes from the Stock Exchange's barrow-boy, who was known as a jobber and who stood, or squatted on a high stool, by his pitch.

Although this system is no longer in use in London, it is still practised in many of the world's markets. So it may be instructive to understand how it worked. Let us assume, for the purpose of this example, that the dealer was seeking to buy shares in British Petroleum.

Without disclosing whether he was a potential buyer or seller, the dealer would seek a quote on BP's price. The jobber, in this example, replied '£5.36 to £5.40', indicating he would buy BP shares at the lower price or sell them at the higher. The gap provided the jobber's 'turn' or margin, in other words, his livelihood. With a share as well known as BP, the jobber would more probably have answered 'thirty-six to forty', correctly assuming that any dealer would have known that the price was in the area of £5.

The dealer would then visit other stalls, much as a cost-conscious shopper might seek the best price for a cauliflower, and obtain alternative quotes. Having settled on the most attractive, and still without disclosing whether he was a buyer or a seller, the dealer then reapproached one of the jobbers, reminded him of the quote he had made a few minutes earlier, and asked if there was a possibility of 'anything closer'.

The jobber, sensing the possibility of an imminent deal, would try to guess whether his client was a buyer or seller, and would then ask: 'Are you many?'. 'Only 500', said the broker, in the knowledge that small packages were usually attractive to jobbers, who, at the end of the trading account, have to balance up buyers with sellers. 'I'll make you thirty-six to thirty-nine and a half,' the jobber replied. In turn the broker said: 'I'll sell you 500 at thirty-six,' and a 'bargain' is struck. This would be recorded on a slip of paper in the notebook of each party.

Under Stock Exchange etiquette, the broker was obliged to deal at the time of the quote, he could not have returned ten minutes later, having haggled elsewhere. Had he decided not to deal, the jobber would have said formally: 'I'm off,' indicating that the quote was no longer valid.

The End of an Era

To some the well-established method of buying and selling shares through jobbers via brokers seemed eternal. After all, as we have seen, it offered the benefit of a truly constant market. Buyers and their brokers did not have to wait hours or even days before finding someone willing to sell them shares. The cut-and-thrust nature of jobbing was there to make sure that fair, competitive prices were always available, while the rule requiring all deals to pass through jobbers prevented brokers from selling stock to customers at artificial high prices. It was also cheap, for jobbers' margins were reasonable, especially for small parcels of stock where little risk was involved.

But market forces and modern technology were threatening this system even before its abolition in October 1986, an event that came to be known as Big Bang. Such had been the impact of taxation and inflation on individual savings in the 1960s and 1970s that the private investor was all but lost to the market, leaving the power, and the money, with the pensions and savings funds. These institutional investors did not see why they should pay fixed broking commissions, which could run into tens of thousands of pounds, for a simple deal that could as well be conducted by telephone. They did not see the need for the brokers' research, since they had their own staff of fund managers and analysts. And as, increasingly, they wanted to buy large parcels of stock, they, or rather their brokers, found the jobbers hard-pressed to find it from their own books and even less willing to take a big risk with the price.

So the institutions started dealing among themselves. They were also helped by a computerized system called Ariel, which was set up by the merchant banks so that fund managers could be kept in touch with transactions and prices as bargains were struck. Soon, knowing the price, fund managers were using Ariel to trade.

It was only a matter of time before what has been termed the dual-dealing system cracked. Stockbrokers began taking shares in firms of stockjobbers, and vice versa. The final push for change came when the Government's Office of Fair Trading brought a legal action against the Stock Exchange, charging that the practice of fixed commissions was unfair, and against the public interest. Without the prop of high commissions from trading between institutions, the single-capacity dealing system, as it was called, was doomed.

A Spectacle Removed

In London the Stock Exchange could have removed the dual-dealing system without abandoning trading on the floor. The world's two largest stock exchanges, New York and Tokyo, both still maintain a huge trading room, where most business is conducted every day, although it is supplemented by electronic trading.

London chose to move to an all-electronic system, modelled on the United States over-the-counter trading market, called NASDAQ, which is described later. At the time of writing Britain has the only national exchange which is all-electronic and is the only major industrialized country where it is not possible for students and members of the public to go to see the stock market at work. Until this change small queues of visitors used to form each day outside the Throgmorton Street headquarters of the London Stock Exchange to be taken on a 'tour', where smartly dressed female guides would show a short film *My Word is My Bond*, deliver a homily on the benefits of capitalism, and conduct parties to a large gallery from which the onlookers could watch millions of shares being bought and sold.

But even though the trading floor is no longer used, today's exchange, operating electronically in the dealing rooms of a score or more large security houses like BZW, has not abolished all links with the past. Some of the nomenclature has changed, but in many respects the jobs are the same.

Firms of sharebrokers are now incorporated, and known, more pretentiously, as securities houses, though those that work in them prefer to call themselves stockbrokers. In fact the person we used to call a stockbroker is now billed as a salesman, while the former stock-jobbers have become market-makers.

But unlike the old stockbroker, today's salesman seldom has time to socialize with those who wish to invest in shares. Most of his clients are institutions, not private investors. Almost all business is conducted on the telephone. The salesman rarely has time to go out for lunch. As the head salesman at BZW put it: 'You get your buzz by doing deals. When you no longer get the buzz you should be out of the business. Lunch is for wimps'.

2. History

*'The howling of the wolf, the grunting of the hog,
the braying of the ass, the nocturnal wooing of the
cat, all these in unison could not be more hideous than
the noise which these beings make in the Stock
Exchange'* – Anonymous commentator on the scene
in Change Alley, London in 1695.

*'Stock-jobbing is knavish in its private practice, and
treason in its public'* – Daniel Defoe.

'Dictum meum pactum – My word is my bond' –
Handbook of the London Stock Exchange.

For most the stock markets epitomize the concept of risk
and reward. With not too much of the former, and the
chance of achieving a fair amount of the latter, the investor
can be on the road to riches. This has been true throughout
the three centuries of stock market activity.

Those who took a billion pound risk in investing in satellite
television in Britain in 1990 were opting for the same choice
as the few backers prepared to chance £3,200 apiece on the
Concepcion adventure in 1686. Then, a whiskery sea captain
from Boston called Phips sought investors for an expedition
to the north-coast of Hispaniola to salvage a sunken galleon.
Nine months later the backers reaped their reward –
£250,000 worth of fine silver. We shall have to wait and see
whether the shareholders of British Sky Broadcasting achieve
a similar return.

Then as now another major threat to any investment has
been that people cheat. There are big cheats and little cheats,
of course, and only a few of them have passed through the
cells of the Old Bailey. The excitement that greeted the trial
in London of the Guinness Five in 1990 or the humiliation
of the president of the House of Nomura a year later – or
the imprisonment that year of Ivan Boesky and Michael

Milken in New York, and Ronald Li in Hong Kong – was only a latter-day repeat of events in Britain in the late seventeenth century.

In 1697, following a wave of market-rigging and insider-trading, the British Government brought in an Act designed to 'restrain the number and ill-practice of brokers and stockjobbers'.

This followed a report from a Parliamentary Commission set up a year earlier which had discovered that:

> the pernicious art of stockjobbing hath, of late, so perverted the end design of Companies and Corporations, erected for the introducing or carrying on of manufactures, to the private profit of the first projectors, that the privileges granted to them have commonly been made no other use of – but to sell again, with advantage, to innocent men.

As a result of the 1697 Act all stockbrokers and stockjobbers had to be licensed before they plied their trade in the coffee shops, walks and alleys near the Royal Exchange in London. These licences were limited to 100 and were granted by the Lord Mayor of London and the Court of Aldermen. They cost only £2, and entitled the licensee to wear a specially struck silver medal embossed with the Royal Arms, once he had taken an oath that he would 'truly and faithfully execute and perform the office and employment of a broker between party and party, without fraud or collusion'.

The rules of operation were strict. Brokers were not allowed to deal on their own behalf, but only for clients. They could not hold any options for more than three days without facing the certainty of permanent expulsion. Commission was limited to 5 per cent, or less. Anyone who tried to operate as a broker without a licence was, if caught, exposed to three days in the City pillory.

Muscovy and Company

The trade in shares had started with City traders and merchants spreading the risk of two major entrepreneurial journeys: an attempt to investigate the prospects offered by the unchartered White Sea and Arctic Circle, and a voyage to India and the East Indies via the Cape of Good Hope.

These ventures were to lead to the world's first two public companies: the Muscovy Company and the East India Company, whose members did not follow previous practice of trading on their own account as private individuals, but contributed money to 'joint stock', through shares which were freely transferable.

The Muscovy Company emerged from a brave, if unsuccessful attempt by Sebastian Cabot in 1553 to find a North East trade route to China and the Orient. As one of the first shareholders explained at the time:

> Every man willing to bee of the societie, should disburse the portion of twentie and five pounds a piece: so that in a short time, by this means, the sum of six thousand pounds being gathered, three ships were brought.

Two of the three ships sank off Norway, and things looked bleak for the 250 merchants putting up £27 each. But one of the project leaders did make it to Moscow, where he persuaded Ivan the Terrible to sign a trade agreement.

The East India Company was more successful and was the first to raise equity capital on a substantial scale. It needed modern, armed ships for the difficult and dangerous voyage to the Orient, and substantial docks in London. Although it lost ships on voyages, and hovered close to bankruptcy, it managed to raise over £1.6m. in 17 years. As the silk and spice trade developed, those who had invested in the original stock saw profit returns of 40 per cent a year.

Enterprising developers quickly realized that raising capital through shares had potential far beyond risky voyages. Why not try it at home? Francis, Earl of Bedford had a bold plan to drain the Fens, which would provide more fertile agricultural land as well as giving London its first supply of fresh water. So others topped up his own £100,000 contribution and 'The Government and Company of the New River brought from Chadwell and Amwell to London' was founded in 1609, to become Britain's first water stock. Although the water company operations were bought out by the Metropolitan Water Board in 1904, the company still exists as the oldest one quoted on the Stock Exchange.

The Stock Exchange Official List

By the end of the seventeenth century there was substantial dealing in shares of one sort or another. It was estimated by the historian W. R. Scott that by 1695 there were some 140 joint stock companies, with a total market capitalization of £4.5m. More by habit than by design, much of this took place in two coffee houses called Garraway's and Jonathan's near Change Alley, which still exists in the narrow spit of land between Cornhill and Threadneedle Street. The coffee establishments of the seventeenth century had style. You could meet there fellow merchants and traders, discuss the latest ventures, and buy and sell shares. You could also run your eye down a sheet of paper containing prices of commodities and a few shares – called 'The Course of the Exchange and Other Things'; this was to be the precursor of the Stock Exchange Daily Official List.

A writer of the day set the scene:

> The centre of the jobbing is in the Kingdom of Exchange Alley and its adjacencies: the limits are easily surrounded in about a Minute and a half stepping out of Jonathan's into the Alley, you turn your face full South, moving on a few paces, and then turning Due East, you advance to Garaway's; from there going out at the other Door, you go on still East into Birchin Lane and then halting a little at the Sword-Blade Bank to do much mischief in fervent Words, you immediately face to the North, enter Cornhill, visit two or three petty Provinces there in your way West; and thus having Boxed your Compass, and sail'd round the whole Stock Jobbing Globe, you turn into Jonathan's again; and so, as most of the great Follies of Life oblige us to do, you end just where you began.

South Sea Bubble

This coffee society was to thrive for more than 50 years, and by 1720 Change Alley, and its coffee houses thronged with

brokers, was the place to be. The narrow streets were impass-
able because of the throng of lords and ladies in their car-
riages. The Act regulating and restricting their operations
had lapsed, by popular consent. And the eighteenth-century
equivalent of the hit parade contained the following ballad:

> Then stars and garters did appear
> Among the meaner rabble
> To buy and sell, to see and hear
> The Jews and Gentiles squabble,
> The greatest ladies thither came
> And plied in chariots daily,
> Or pawned their jewels for a sum
> To venture in the Alley.

The principal attraction was the excitement caused by the
booming share prices of the South Sea Company, which
started in 1720 at £128 apiece, and swiftly rose as euphoria
about their prospects was spread both by brokers and by the
Government. By March the price rose to £330, by May it
was £550, and by 24 June it had reached an insane £1,050.

The South Sea Company had been set up nine years earlier
by the British Government, ostensibly with the aim of opening up trade and markets for new commodities in South
America. It also had another purpose, which, these days, has
a familiar ring about it, for it was to relieve the Government
of some £9m. of public debt.

For eight years it did virtually nothing, and created no
excitement. Its shares were static, and it had only one contract of any size: to supply black slaves to Latin America. The
Government then gave birth to the concept of privatization of
a State concern, something much more audacious than the
contemporary sales of British Telecom or British Gas. It
offered shares in the South Sea Company to the public,
hoping that it would raise enough money to wipe out the
entire National Debt of some £31m.

The Government was persuaded to do this by a wily operator, Sir John Blunt, who was a director of the company and
effectively underwrote the issue. The issues were 'partly-
paid'; an investor had to find only a small proportion at the
start, and then pay the rest of the share price in instalments.

The issue was heavily oversubscribed, and there was much irritation when it was discovered that Blunt's acquaintances, and others of influence, had received an extra allocation. To raise still more money, the company made loans to the public, secured on the shares themselves, provided the money was used to buy more stock. Blunt also proved adept at the use of public relations in pushing the share price up. There were promises of lavish dividends, the interest of prominent people was secured by thinly veiled bribes, and the peace negotiations with Spain were used for propaganda purposes, since the prospect of an end to conflict meant more trade with South America.

The smart money, including the Prime Minister, Sir Robert Walpole, sold out at the peak of the boom. The Prince of Wales, the Duke of Argyll, the Chancellor of the Exchequer and MPs too numerous to mention, made handsome gains before the bubble burst. Then the Government, by bringing in the Bubble Act, designed to prevent a rash of similar competitive enterprises from springing up, triggered off the first ever bear market. So the bubble burst, and within eight weeks of passing £1,000, the share price had plunged to £175. By December it had sunk to £124, bringing ruin to those who had seen the South Sea Company as the chance of a lifetime. There was the inevitable Parliamentary inquiry, which concluded that the accounts had been falsified and a government minister bribed. The Chancellor had no chance to enjoy his £800,000 capital gain; he was committed to the Tower after being found guilty of the 'most notorious, dangerous and infamous corruption'.

It was – and remains – the most notorious episode in British financial history, and it was a long time before the market got back into its stride. Indeed it was not until the next century that a large crop of joint stock companies was formed, a development brought about by an acute shortage of capital for major projects both at home and abroad.

Mines, Railways, Canals

By 1824, the end of the cyclical trade depression, there were 156 companies quoted on the London Stock Exchange, with a market capitalization of £47.9m. In the following twelve months interest in investment increased sharply. Prospectuses were issued for no less than 624 companies with capital requirements of £372m. The largest group were general investment companies, mostly with extensive interests overseas, which raised £52m. Canals and railways came next, raising £44m., followed by mining companies, £38m. and insurance, a new industry, with £35m.

The railways proved a great boon for the promotion of investment, even if most of the investors lost their shirts. The Duke of Wellington had opposed the development of railways: 'Railroads will only encourage the lower classes to move about needlessly'. Not only did this prove to be the case, but investment in the railways also led to the spread of share ownership outside London and the ruling classes to the provinces. It also created a new word in the financial vocabulary: stag, a person who applied for an allotment of shares with the clear intention of selling them to someone else before he has to pay for them.

The stags were out in force in 1836 when George Hudson, a bluff Yorkshireman, raised £300,000 for the York and North Midland Railway under the slogan 'Mak' all t'railways coom t'York'. The £50 shares were oversubscribed and quickly gained a premium of £4 each. Within three years the line was opened, and the bells of York Minster pealed out in joyful celebration. Much of the joy was shortlived, however, for so many railway lines sprouted up across the country that many of them could not pay the wages of the train drivers, let alone the dividends. Many of them also turned out to be overcapitalized, with the surplus funds vanishing into other ventures, to the shareholders' chagrin.

Even so, despite setbacks, by 1842 there were 66 railway companies quoted on the London Stock Exchange, with a capital of almost £50m. During the boom in railway issues, *The Economist* was moved to write an editorial, which, with the change of name and date, might well have fitted into the British Telecom era of 1985: 'Everybody is in the stocks now (sic),' it purred. 'Needy clerks, poor tradesmen's apprentices, discarding serving men and bankrupts – all have entered the ranks of the great moneyed interest.'

Provincial stock markets were also being established. Local

investment opportunities had been featured in the advertisements of share auctions which regularly appeared in the
Liverpool newspapers after about 1827. It was quite usual
to use a property auction as the opportunity to dispose of a
parcel of shares. By the middle of 1845 regional stock
exchanges had been formed in 12 towns and cities, from
Bristol in the South, to Newcastle in the North, with York-
shire claiming the greatest number. But only five of them
survived the trading slump of 1845 to become permanent
institutions.

Government Debt

All through this period government debt had been growing,
and its funding was providing the most lucrative and reliable
form of income to sharebrokers. In 1860, British funds
amounted to more than all the other quoted securities combined, and provided by far the widest market in the
Exchange. Compensation to slave-owners, whose slaves had
been freed, the cost of the Crimean War and the purchase
by the Government of the national telegraph system, all
added to the cost.

Government stocks, or bonds, were bought daily from the
Treasury by the City figure called the Government Broker,
who then sold them on in the market-place. The idea was
that these stocks, to become known much later as gilt-edged
securities, would be used to cut back or even get rid of the
National Debt. In effect, of course, they added to the debt,
but they were a way of funding unpopular measures without
resorting to excessive taxation. By the early twentieth century
local authorities had also jumped on the bandwagon. The
City of Dublin was the first to raise money through bonds,
followed by Edinburgh, Glasgow and the Metropolitan
Board of Works.

The First Exchange

The brokers and other money dealers had, of course, long
since left their damp pitches in Change Alley, and the coffee

shops had not only become too crowded but also too accommodating to groups which the more established professionals
liked to call the 'riff-raff'. When Jonathan's was finally burnt
down after a series of major fires around 1748, the broking
industry sought refuge in New Jonathan's, rebuilt in Threadneedle Street, where they charged sixpence a day entrance
fee, a sum sufficient to discourage tinkers, money-lenders
and the other parasites that had frequented the previous
premises. Soon afterwards they put a sign over the door: The
Stock Exchange.

It continued in this way, more or less as a club, for 30
years, until its members decided something more formal was
required. On 7 February 1801 its days as the Stock Exchange
ended and it was shut down, to reopen one month later as
the 'Stock Subscription Room'. It no longer cost sixpence a
day to enter; members had to be elected and to pay a fee of
ten guineas, and risk a fine of two guineas if they were found
guilty of 'disorderly conduct', the penalty going to charity.
There does not seem to be an accurate record of how much
charities benefited from this provision. The Stock Subscription Room had a short life, for members quickly decided it
was too small, and in the same year laid the foundation stone
for a new building in Capel Court. The stone records that
this was also the 'first year of the union between Great
Britain and Ireland', and notes that the building was being
'erected by private subscription for transaction of the business in the public funds'.

Not all members of the public were impressed by this new
monument; the old lady who sold cups of tea and sweet
buns outside Capel Court moved away because, she said: 'the
Stock Exchange is such a wicked place'. But with monuments
come tablets, and it was not long before members were
forced to draw up new rules of operation. Adopted in 1812,
these still form the basis of the present-day rule book. Neither
members nor their wives could be engaged in any other
business, failures had to be chalked up above the clock
immediately so that there could be a fair distribution of
assets to creditors, and members were informed that they
had to give up 'rude and trifling practices which have long
disgraced the Stock Exchange'.

The Capel Court building was to last a century and a half,

and it was, in the end, not size but ancient communications that made it unworkable. The decision was taken to rebuild, and the present London Stock Exchange occupies a 321-feet high, 26-storey tower. Until October 1986, when trading on the floor ceased, you could visit the gallery of the Exchange and watch the excitement and bustle below. But those days are gone: the computer and the telephone have taken over.

3   The Footsie and the Dow

'It was like a Franz Kafka novel, trying to plan the future of one of our great national institutions, without knowing what was in store.' – Sir Nicholas Goodison, former Chairman of the Stock Exchange.

'The main impact of the Big Bang has been an unprecedented and unholy game of musical chairs. Instead of a Who's Who, the City badly needs a Who's Where?' – Robert Heller, publisher and writer.

The City of London, a damp and unprepossessing square mile of grey stone and cement built on mudflats at the mouth of Britain's river Thames, has been the world's most important financial influence since the days of the cargo cult. It is a great survivor. London Bridge may have burned down, but the City survived the holocaust of the Great Fire. Warring armies skirmished in what are now known as the Home Counties, but never scaled the City's walls. Hitler's Blitz left the Square Mile badly scarred but trading continued amid the sirens and the firefighting. When invasion seemed imminent, many City men packed their wives and children off to the Welsh hills or to country farmsteads, but stayed at their desks, minding the nation's money shop.

The City, almost miraculously, also survived Britain's postwar economic and political decline. While heavy industry crumbled – and much of manufacturing industry has had to fight for survival – the banks and other financial institutions that provide most of Britain's invisible exports have thrived and prospered. Britain is still merchant banker to the free world, and foreign governments, corporations and individual potentates daily entrust gold, silver and dollars to financial houses in the City of London.

Each day about £50 billion worth of foreign currency changes hands in London, yielding the banks and exchange dealers a fortune in commission, and making the City the dominant market in foreign exchange.

The City is a complacent kind of place, and, like much of Britain, often resistant to change. Administratively it is run by a Corporation, which controls a square mile area fanning out from a six-road junction overlooked by the Bank of England, the Royal Exchange and the Mansion House. The Corporation of London, which has no responsibilities in the capital beyond the square mile, is the only council in the United Kingdom which is not democratically elected. The City elders, or aldermen, are chosen not by those who live or work in the area, but by livery companies and other privileged groups, representing, for the most part, the establishment.

Yet the City has muddled through, and until the autumn of 1986 operated well enough on a mixture of trust, jousting and spirited rivalry. The combination of events which came to be known as Big Bang were seen to offer the dawning of a new age of opportunity, but in fact backfired and presented it with new challenges and threats which it has still to meet. As rents spiralled and wage bills soared many firms lost money, and are still on thin profit margins. Much is at stake: almost one million people are employed in the finance industry in the Greater London area, the biggest percentage in the City, where rents are much higher than elsewhere in Europe.

In 1991, having failed to meet the challenges offered by information technology to reduce communications costs and increase efficiency, the Corporation of London indulged in one of its periodic phases of navel-gazing, and raised £1.5 million for an investigation by the London Business School into its competitiveness. The LBS study, headed by Professor Richard Brealey, will make comparisons with New York, Tokyo, Frankfurt and Paris. But it will not report back until 1994.

This seems like a recipe to postpone further essential change, but all the evidence from the past is that the City, when threatened, rises to the occasion. At a basic level, when the British Government sought to build a second city in the reclaimed Docklands area a few miles to the east, offering rents at a fraction of City prices, the Corporation suddenly found it possible to relax its planning regulations, and construction work proliferated.

A much more sustained assault has been mounted by Labour politicians.

For the best part of three decades, large sections of the Labour movement – and not only the Left – attacked the City with the kind of passion that comes when hatred is mixed with envy. Labour Governments have threatened the City with reform, perhaps even overthrow, and those at the centre of the Labour Party have not shied from expressing emotive desires – for instance, Denis Healey's wish to squeeze and squeeze 'until the pips squeak'. Socialist desires to bring the City to heel in the 60s and 70s resulted in there being an almost continuous state of inquiry into the activities of the Square Mile. But despite the probing of the commissions of inquiry chaired by Lord Radcliffe and Lord Wilson, the City, until 1986, remained intact, and largely responsible for policing its own affairs. Although innumberable scandals have at times appeared to threaten its independence, it has managed until now to avoid coming under the supervision of a powerful Securities and Exchange Commission, such as exists in the United States.

To be sure, the regulatory regime is much tougher than it used to be, and the government has established the Securities and Investment Board (SIB) to try to ensure fair play – but the activities of the board are funded by the financial services industry not the taxpayer, and most of the rules have been drawn up by the practitioners.

On the surface, then, at the end of the 80s, with a friendly if headstrong Conservative government in power at Westminster and left-wing politics confined to decaying urban boroughs, the City is thriving. There is visible evidence of prosperity at every corner. At lunchtime the best restaurants are usually booked, despite the high prices, while a new breed of City worker may be seen quaffing champagne and munching smoked salmon sandwiches in a brief respite from the desk.

Despite the problems, and some outmoded attitudes, the City still has much in its favour. Its most important asset is its unrivalled geographical position, right on the earth's central meridian. London sits on Greenwich Mean Time, and so operates in the middle of the world's trading day. London is open when business in Tokyo, Hong Kong and Sydney is winding down. Londoners are still at their desks when trading in Wall Street begins. They also speak English, the global business language.

London is also easily accessible. Its major airports provide the most important international airline hub. International telecommunications are good, even though they fall down at local level. Britain may no longer have an empire, but the traditions of trade, entrepreneurship and exploitation that brought the country such financial success after the Industrial Revolution, have lingered on. Londoners are international in their outlook, and prefer a deregulated environment.

That being so, even though the British economy now rates low down in the top twelve, behind France and Italy, and although the size of the British equities market is dwarfed by those of New York or Tokyo, London still boasts the most important and only true international market. In London you can trade the shares of nearly all the world's most important companies. In this respect the international market in London provides a true barometer to the health of the world's capitalist system.

London is an important centre of more than 600 banks from 70 countries: mainly because it is the headquarters of the multi-trillion dollar foreign exchange and Eurobond markets. It is also the most important centre for investment banking, commercial law, and international accountancy.

The Eurobond Market

On the Eurobond market any large and creditable multinational corporation can now borrow money on a global scale by issuing bonds – fixed interest securities denominated in a currency of its choice repayable over a long period.

Buying and selling international bonds is a natural development of international currency trading. For years currencies have been traded against each other by telephone, with active markets in all the financial centres mentioned earlier. The end of restrictions on the flow of money in and out of currencies led to the explosive growth of what are now known as the Euromarkets. These grew from the trade in American dollars, whose owners had no desire to repatriate them to the United States. They therefore provided a pool of money for investment outside North America. The Euro-dollar market gave birth to the European market; and now the Euromarkets embrace a host of other currencies, as well as hybrids such as the European Currency Unit, or ECU.

It was only a short time before straightforward currency loans developed into bond finance, as foreign governments, multinational agencies and large corporations found it con-venient to borrow from this pool of money. Now the Euro-bond market is very large and very sophisticated. Trans-national corporations in particular find Eurobonds a tax-efficient way of raising money. They set up subsidiaries in Luxembourg or the Netherlands Antilles to issue them, and back the bonds with the guarantee not only of their own international reputation, but also that of the group of mer-chant banks or finance houses who act as underwriters. The money raised can be switched to any part of the world where the company needs it.

One advantage, at least for some of those who invest in Eurobonds, is their anonymity. There is no central register, which inquisitive journalists or private detectives may scruti-nize, in order to establish a bondholder's wealth. Bonds are obtained from the register of the company or government issuing them, usually via the dealer.

Eurobonds are much favoured by investors in European countries with high personal taxation. Because they are issued in bearer, rather than registered, form they are anony-mous, and interest is paid free of any local withholding tax. Wealthy professionals, notably dentists in Belgium, buy them, taking the train or driving to Luxembourg at dividend time to collect the tax-free funds, and depositing their income in a Swiss or Luxembourg bank.

Some of these securities are what are called zero-coupon bonds: that is they do not pay any interest, but are available at a discount to their final value. For instance the Alliance and Leicester Building Society raised money from the Euro-bond market. In June 1990 you could buy in the secondary market its 1995 bonds for a 50 per cent discount on its redemption. In other words if you invested £50 you would be guaranteed £100 in December 1995, not a bad return assuming inflation continues at below 10 per cent a year.

New Eurobond issues are not for the private investor. The first that most investors know about a new bond issue is after it has taken place, when an advertisement – known as a 'tombstone' because of its shape and general greyness – appears in *The Financial Times* and *The Wall Street Journal*. One recent tombstone announced that Heron International Finance NV, registered in The Hague, had issued ECU 60m. 9⅜ per cent guaranteed retractable bonds, repayable between 1992 and 1997. The bonds, said the tombstone, would be 'unconditionally guaranteed jointly and severally' by Heron International NV, of Curaçao in the Netherlands Antilles, and Heron International plc, of London. Beneath this statement was a list of banks. Three of them, Banque Indosuez, Banque Bruxelles Lambert SA and Lloyds Merchant Bank Ltd were displayed across the top of the list. Beneath were the names of 18 more banks, five of them European, four American, four Japanese, and three British.

What this advertisement told the reader familiar with these tombstones was that Gerald Ronson's Heron Group had raised a sum of money equivalent to 60m. European Currency Units of Account – about £33m. – by issuing bonds at just under 10 per cent interest. In the months ahead if general interest rates were to go down, the value of the bonds would go up, because of the yield, and vice versa. The three lead banks named had organized the capital raising, and, with the other banks listed, were guaranteeing to find buyers. In fact, even before the advertisement appeared, bond salesmen at each of the banks would have contacted major institutional investors offering parcels of the bonds for sale.

In the same issue of *The Financial Times*, tombstones reported an ECU 100m. issue for the French nuclear power utility Centrale Nucléaire Européenne à Neutrons Rapides SA at 9 per cent, $500m. for the International Bank for Reconstruction and Development, and $75m, for Japan's Sumitomo Chemical Company.

Belying their name, the Euromarkets are nothing whatever to do with the European Community, and although the European Currency Unit has its attractions as a denominator currency, it is dwarfed in volume by bonds denominated in other currencies, such as the US dollar, the German Mark, or the Japanese yen. Nor is most of the action in Continental Europe; the centre for Euromarket activity is London. There is, however, no trading floor, and almost all the business is carried out by telephone, with the major Eurobond dealers working from large electronic dealing rooms. Nor are the principal operators British, but American and Swiss, with three groups dominant – Merrill Lynch, Goldman Sachs and Crédit Suisse First Boston.

Unfortunately for the Stock Exchange most of this activity totally by-passed it, much to its chagrin. An even greater irritation was the introduction of a new instrument – the equity-convertible Eurobond – whereby a company raised loan finance through the issue of a ten-year interest-bearing bond, but gave the bond-holder the option of retrieving his capital through the allocation of equities in the company. Thus shares in both British and international companies were issued in large quantities without any stock market getting a sniff of the deal.

Commercial Paper

Another development which has by-passed stockmarkets has been the development of a commercial paper market, both on a global and British scale, brought about because large and prestigious corporations realized that the cost of short-term borrowing through the banking system was far too high. Why pay high interest rates, they asked themselves, when they could borrow directly from investment institutions who would be only too pleased to lend them surplus funds short-term? After all many commercial multinationals could be considered a safer bet than banks, with their record of misjudgment on Third World loans.

Commercial paper in fact is not much more than IOU's – backed by the good name of the corporation or country issuing the IOU. It is offered to investors at a discount which reflects current interest rates, and on maturity, which is usually over a period of between one month and one year, the investor gets back the full value of the note. There is no shortage of investors. Those who have a few spare million dollars – often themselves cash rich corporations – believe that having certificates issued by companies like IBM, Ford or General Motors is as good a short-term security as anything else, and if they want to get their money back before the IOU is payable there is a secondary market in which they can do this. In the United States the commercial paper market is worth over $300 billion, accounting for nearly one fifth of all private debt. By comparison, the Eurocommercial paper market, usually denominated in dollars, is a fledgling, but over 100 major companies each year use it to raise short-term capital totalling about $80 billion. A more recent development has been a sterling commercial paper market, which, as its name implies, is for those companies, mostly British, that wish to raise funds in pounds.

Although the purpose of commercial paper is to raise short-term finance, many programmes are rolled over at the end of the life of the issue, with perhaps a new rate negotiated. Some commercial paper issues offer the possibility of converting the paper to equity at the expiry of the note. This is a cheap way of making a share issue, and it enables the company to tap international institutions without resorting to the normal procedures, by-passing the stock markets.

The Big Bang

October 1986 was the most momentous month in the long history of the London Stock Exchange – a combination of forces for change known as Big Bang. One force was Margaret Thatcher: in her assault on trades unions' restrictive practices she determined that fixed commissions charged by stockbrokers should be abolished, and that all major financial institutions should have free and open access to the capital markets. The principal barriers between banks, merchant banks, investment institutions and stockbrokers should be broken down: all should be able to set up as one-stop financial supermarkets if they wished to. Why not allow one company to buy and sell shares for clients, raise capital for business, invest in new ventures, and trade in international securities like Eurobonds?

But by far the biggest force for change was technology:

the combination of hi-speed telecommunications and the microprocessor meant that international deals could be carried out anywhere. There was no need for any of the very large trades to pass through the Stock Exchange at all.

Immediately prior to Big Bang 62 per cent of the trading in one of Britain's largest companies, ICI, was being transacted off the London Exchange, mainly in New York. A large share of the buying and selling of other major British companies had also been taking place in the United States. This trading was by no means confined to American investors, for some of the big British institutions found that dealing across the Atlantic was a better proposition. An official of the Prudential Assurance Company explained; 'When we have a significant buying programme on we check all available markets. We take the attitude that we deal wherever we can get the best price.'

In other words the big traders saw no need to deal in London, where the complicated system of brokers and jobbers was costing them much more in commission, government stamp duty and Value Added Tax.

So, for Sir Nicholas Goodison, Chairman of the Stock Exchange and his colleagues on the Council, sweeping reform was the only answer. If the Stock Exchange were to compete with the giant American broking houses, it had to join them at their own game. There was no choice, when competition was creaming off the top business, both in value and volume. Otherwise there would be nothing left for the old-fashioned Stock Exchange, and the jobbers would be left standing at their pitches.

Effecting the necessary changes took time and considerable resolution. It meant ending a way of life that had been a tradition for more than 100 years. It meant abolishing a system that had secured a good income for thousands of people working for stockbrokers.

Even though its members saw the system was under threat, the Stock Exchange Council had to be given a firm nudge in the direction of change by the Government. This happened almost by accident. The Office of Fair Trading had argued that stockbrokers should be treated no differently from other sectors of the community – solicitors, estate agents, motor traders, soap powder manufacturers – who had been barred from fixing prices amongst each other, and were now bound to offer some semblance of competition in the market place. When the Stock Exchange demurred, the Government decided to take legal action, using the weight of the Monopolies Commission to take apart the entire rule book of the Exchange as a litany of restrictive practices. The proceedings were estimated to take five years to complete, and to cost at least £5m. in legal fees. It was, of course, using a sledgehammer to crack a nut and an absurd way of challenging an entire trading system. As Sir Nicholas Goodison, chairman at the time, was to say later:

'It was a foolish way to study the future of a great international market. It was a matter which needed long and close study, and preferably a public examination not constrained by the requirements of litigation or the straitjacket of court procedure. Unfortunately the Government turned down the suggestion of such an examination, and we were forced into a position of defence of rules, not all of which we would necessarily wish to keep. This open debate became impossible because anything said could, as it were, be taken down in evidence and used in court. The case preempted resources, effort and thought.'

It did, however, concentrate the mind of the Stock Exchange Council. The Government was clearly in no mood to set up a Royal Commission to inquire into the Stock Exchange; Ministers saw that as a waste of time. If the case went on, with each side producing volumes of written evidence, as well as witnesses for examination, cross-examination and re-examination, the Stock Exchange would end up in an unwinnable situation. There would also be unfavourable publicity. And even if the Exchange won, its joy would be shortlived, for such was the resolve of the Thatcher Government to curb the restrictive power of trades unions that it could hardly spare as notorious a City club, and would then feel obliged to legislate to change the law.

In July 1983 the Government offered Sir Nicholas Goodison a way out. It offered to drop the case against the Stock Exchange, if the Council would abandon fixed commissions. It did so, and the die was cast for Big Bang.

Both the Government and the Stock Exchange knew that the abolition of fixed commissions would be the catalyst for major change, because without steady reliance on a solid income, more or less indexed to the rate of inflation, many stockbrokers could not exist. Competition over commissions might be acceptable in a bull market, but when the bears emerged in strength there would be trouble. A bull is the name for the optimist who believes that prices are likely to go higher, and who charges into the market to buy; if there are enough bulls, their confidence is sufficient to push up prices. A bear is the opposite market animal, who fears the worst, and expects a fall; when the bears run for cover, you have a bear market. For stockbrokers, a bear market generates fear, for although there are good commissions to be had when there is pronounced selling, the prices on which those commissions are based are lower, and interest dies.

An end to fixed commissions altogether would mean a change in the way of life for most brokers, and the Old Guard did not like it. Life was cosy on a fixed commission. Costs had gone up, but so had the rate of commission. In 1950 the commission on the purchase or sale of ordinary shares had been a sliding scale falling to 0.5 per cent for larger trades. According to Messrs Basil, Montgomery, Lloyd and Ward's pocket guide, a share valued at 15s. (at the old rate of 20 shillings to the pound and 12 pence to a shilling) would then cost the investor 15s 5¼d., after paying stamp duty of 3¾d, and commission of 1½d. A £5 share would cost £5. 2s. 9d., with the broker getting 9d. for his pains. By 1952 commission rates had gone up – to 0.75 per cent for large trades, but the 15s. share still cost the investor only ¾d. more at 15s 6d., while the £5 share cost him £5. 3s., with the broker getting a whole shilling instead of 9d. for the trade. Ten years later the rates were much higher at 1.25 per cent, but in the case of transactions of over £2,500, the broker could, at his discretion, reduce the commission for the surplus to not less than half the standard rate, provided the business was not shared with an agent, in which case the full rate had to be charged. On February 24 1975 there was another rise – to 1.5 per cent for the first £5,000 consideration, falling to 0.625 per cent for the next £15,000. Decimalization had made calculations simpler; the £5 share now cost the investor £5.1625, of which 10p, went in stamp duty and 6.25p. in commission.

On this rate the average broker did not even have to worry overmuch about share prices, because, as we shall see later, jobbers fixed them, and took the risk. There was no need to worry overmuch about losing business to competitors, because there was just about enough to go round, and advertising was banned. You obtained clients through 'connections' and some wining and dining. There was no serious worry about finding and keeping staff because, in the clublike atmosphere of the Stock Exchange, loyalties to individual firms were high. There was little danger to health from overwork. Client interest in shares in North America and the Pacific Basin had extended the working day a little, so an early start was desirable, with a partners' meeting at 8.30, and of course it was no longer possible to catch the 4.48 train home to the stockbroker belt, a group of leafy suburbs in Surrey or Kent. But a good lunch with clients in a private dining room was a compensation, and the weekends could be spent on the golf course.

Under the 'Big Bang', the Old Guard knew, everything would be very different. Those who wanted to survive would have to behave like Chicago futures dealers. Life would become just like a job on the money or commodity markets, with young men and women arriving to a room full of telephones and computer terminals at 7.30 every morning, shouting at them and at each other for at least 12 hours, and leaving exhausted in the evening. This was a world where the mid-life crisis came at the age of 26.

And competition would be so fierce there would probably be less money in it anyway. With no fixed commissions, firms would have neither the time nor the resources to undertake company or sector research, let alone visit a firm and enjoy a steak and kidney pie in a country hotel with the chairman and managing director. Instead they would spend their days peering at monitors, and yelling down the telephone.

As for open ownership, well, the senior partners would sell out, pocket their millions, and go to live in Bermuda, whilst those left would not know who their bosses were, only that they worked for some large bank, almost certainly under foreign ownership.

The Crucial Vote

Despite their defeat over commissions, the Old Guard held out against other reforms. However on 4 June 1985 the 4,495 members of the Stock Exchange were confronted with an historic choice: to face up to the future or face the consequences of living with the past.

Two resolutions were put to the members' vote on the floor of the Exchange. For Sir Nicholas Goodison, the issue was clear. It was about 'whether or not members want to keep the bulk of the securities business in this country and in the Stock Exchange', he wrote in a letter. 'It is about keeping and strengthening the Stock Exchange as the natural market in securities.'

The first resolution, which required only a simple majority, would enable outsiders – banks, mining finance houses, international conglomerates, money brokers – to own up to 100 per cent of a member firm, instead of only 29.9 per cent. The second resolution required a 75 per cent majority, and proposed changes in the Stock Exchange Constitution to shift ownership of the Exchange from individual members to member firms. Plans were to be devised whereby members could sell their shares in the Exchange to newcomers.

The first resolution was passed by 3,246 votes to 681, but the second failed by a very small margin to achieve the required majority, achieving 73.64 per cent instead of the required 75 per cent. For Goodison, this was a major setback, but for those who had voted against it, it was to prove an even greater blow.

Goodison had already warned members that to reject the proposal would be 'very serious and could cause substantial damage to the standing of the Stock Exchange', mainly because new entrants from America and elsewhere, if denied easy membership, would decide simply to by-pass its activities. But Goodison had one major card to play. Under his leadership the Stock Exchange's reputation and credibility had been high. In almost every other area of the City there had been scandal, but the Stock Exchange had retained its integrity, and been shown to be a more effective policeman of those within its province than the Bank of England. Goodison was able to secure the Stock Exchange's right to self-regulation under the Conservative Government's proposed financial services legislation, thus making it certain that those who wished to trade in British equities would want to be governed by its rules. The Exchange's Council then moved to create the new class of corporate membership effective from March 1986.

Corporate members would then each own one share, which gave them the right to take part in all of the Stock Exchange's trading activities, and to use its settlement and other facilities. But there would be no need for any corporate member to have an individual member on either its board or staff, although all those in its employ who had contact with customers would have to be 'approved persons'. Thus, those members who had voted against the Council on the second resolution in the hope of getting better terms for selling their individual shares to new conglomerate members found that these shares were virtually worthless. The biggest group in the world could join the club for only one share, negotiating the price, not with old members, but with the Stock Exchange Council.

The Stock Exchange retained the right to discipline individuals in the new conglomerates, however, even though these individuals were not members. But Goodison did have to make one major concession. Up to March 1986 all members had to take the Stock Exchange examinations. This had to be waived for those working for corporate members, mainly because most of the experienced staff coming under the aegis of the Exchange would be unwilling to take the examinations.

The World's First International Exchange
No sooner had the new deal gone through and the day of 'Big Bang' passed, relatively without incident, than Goodison achieved a major coup. As outlined earlier, one of the major threats to the London Stock Exchange was international equity trading by-passing London altogether. Even though the new rules made London less uncompetitive – and electronic dealing systems forced traders to work faster – there was still a large group of securities houses trading international stocks who saw no good reason why they should be part of the new Exchange.

They had formed themselves into ISRO, the International

Securities Regulatory Organization, which, despite its grandiose title, showed very little affection for regulation. Its members traded in the stocks of about 400 of the world's major corporations for the benefit of about 80 institutions. It was an exclusive club for the big boys, who argued that since they all knew each other not many rules were needed.

Prior to 'Big Bang' ISRO and the London Exchange were not exactly the best of friends; indeed they often traded insults. Since international equities were stocks which were traded beyond their own country boundaries, it was argued they should not be subject to rigid domestic rules. And a new class of international equity was being spawned; issues by international corporations underwritten and distributed in alien countries. The first really large issue of this kind was British Telecom; when it was floated off by the British Government a large proportion of the stock was successfully offered to institutions in North America, Europe and Japan.

Such international equity issues are organized by merchant banks and securities houses who offer tranches of stock directly to favoured clients without touching the stock markets. Because of London's position at the centre of the world business time zone, most of this business has been conducted there. Goodison approached ISRO and suggested that sooner or later some form of ordered regulation for the conduct of global equity markets would be forced on it, if it did not form an international standard of its own; and since the London Stock Exchange offered the nearest to such a standard, why not merge with it?

From the Stock Exchange point of view the proposed deal averted the possibility of the world's financial giants setting up a competing marketplace in London, and, according to Goodison, opened 'the way for a united securities market which will be a very powerful competitor for international business'.

On November 12 1986, members of the Stock Exchange voted for the merger, and the combined body became known as the International Stock Exchange of the United Kingdom and Northern Ireland. The old guard knew there was no choice – the new Exchange was going to be dominated by foreigners, but so what? The previous changes they had approved had already allowed foreign financial houses to take over two-thirds of large British broking firms, and so domination by the likes of Citicorp, American Express, Deutschebank, Merrill Lynch, Nomura, and the Swiss Banking Corporation was anyway inevitable. There was also a sweetener of £10,000 for each member when they retired or reached the age of 60.

The New Conglomerates

The establishment of giant new conglomerates led to an undignified scramble as City and international broking firms, banks and finance houses rushed to jump into bed with each other. So unseemly was the haste that some parted company with new-found, if expensive, friends within days rather than weeks, in a kind of financial promiscuity which must have left old faithfuls gasping for breath. One major bank bought a firm of jobbers only to find that, by the time the ink was dry on the contract, the best people had all left *en masse* to join a rival. Since these people had been almost the firm's only asset, the acquisition was more or less worthless. The Deputy Governor of the Bank of England put his finger on the problem:

> 'If key staff – and on occasions whole teams – can be offered inducements to move suddenly from one institution to another it becomes very difficult for any bank to rely on the commitment individuals will give to implementing its plans, and adds a further dimension of risk to any bank which is building its strategy largely around a few individuals' skills."

The banks and merchant banks were the predators, but they found even the very large broking forms only too willing to submit. Typical of the alliances formed was Barclays De Zoete Wedd, a merger between the investing banking side of Barclays Bank plc, the large stockbrokers, De Zoete and Bevan, and London's largest stockjobber in gilt-edged securities, Wedd, Durlacher & Mordaunt. Barclays became top dog, owning 75 per cent of the shares. Another group was Mercury, formed by S. G. Warburg and Co., with three major broking and jobbing firms. Each of these two giants is able to issue securities, to place them with its large clientele base, and to buy and sell speculatively on its own account.

All but one of Britain's top twenty broking and jobbing

houses were absorbed into large new financial conglomerates. Among the leading firms, only Cazenove and Co.
remained independent. By taking this step, it benefited from
both institutions and private investors seeking out brokers
with no commercial link, and therefore no potential conflict
of interest with a bank, an insurance company or a unit trust
management company.

So were spawned new monoliths which can, in parallel,
act as bankers to a company, raise long-term debt or equity,
make a market in its shares, retail them to investors, and
buy them as managers of discretionary funds. How can the
public be sure that those at the marketing end of the firm
are not privy to insider information, and, if they are, how
can they be prevented from acting upon it? Sensitive information does not, of course, have to be in written form in a
report; a nudge and a wink over lunch is a more subtle,
more common, and less detectable way of passing secrets.
The official Stock Exchange answer to this problem, to be
discussed in greater depth later, is that 'Chinese Walls' must
be erected between the various parts of a financial services
company, so that the interest of the public or investors comes
first.

The arrival of the new monoliths also upset the staid City
career structure. Salaries rocketed as a game of musical chairs
for all but the most mundane jobs got under way. Staffs of
merchant banks and broking firms, whose only regular bright
spot had previously been the annual bonus payment, suddenly found, to their wonderment, that they had taken over
from soccer professionals as the group in society most likely
to be able to bid up earnings without lifting their game. 'The
trick,' one 26–year-old woman employed by a Swiss bank
told me, 'is to always appear to be in demand. If they think
you are about to leave, they will offer more without you
having to ask for it.'

Fast Money

Along with a move towards a super league of financial conglomerates came another major switch of attitudes – an
obsession with short-term performance.

It has become clear that fund managers – the men and
women who manage the money in pension funds, life assur-

ance companies and unit trusts – are no longer prepared to play safe by maintaining large holdings in giant but dull corporations. Not long ago the average institutional investor shared his portfolio between government gilt-edged securities (interest-bearing bonds) and blue-chip equities (shares in well-known companies like Unilever, BP and ICI).

Now they prefer to move their money around, terrifying corporate treasurers who watch, helpless, as large blocks of their companies' shares are traded for what seems fashion or a whim. A fund manager may desert GEC, as many did soon after Big Bang, and buy into Siemens of Germany, IBM of America or Sony of Japan, thereby gambling on future currency movements as well as on the future profitability of a company or market sector. Or he may buy Eurobonds. And because of the risk of volatile movements in exchange or interest rates, he may protect himself by an options or futures contract (of which more later), or both. The result is that fund managers tend towards taking profits whenever they present themselves.

The consequences of this, of course, has been that the companies whose financial performances are, at best, languid cease to have the wholesale support of the institutions, and their share prices fall, making them ripe for takeover.

The Crash of '87

Almost one year after Big Bang there was another momentous event – the Crash of '87. While most people in Britain were repairing damage caused to their homes by the worst hurricane this century, and the media was concentrating on this natural disaster, across the Atlantic another storm was brewing. In the first few hours of trading in Wall Street the Dow Jones Industrial Average had slid 100 points, its biggest ever one-day fall.

Over the next few days we were to witness a drop in equity values as large as the Great Crash of 1929 when bankrupt brokers leapt to their deaths from the skyscrapers of lower Manhattan. This time no one jumped, but one man lost £308 million. 'It's only paper', he said. 'It was paper when we started and it's paper now'. On Black Thursday

October 24 1929 12,894,650 shares had changed hands. And as reported by John Kenneth Galbraith in his book on the Great Crash, most did so at 'prices which shattered the dreams and hopes of those who had owned them'.

The same was true of October 1987. What Galbraith had observed in 1929 was repeated almost to the letter:

'Of all the mysteries of the Stock Exchange, there is none so impenetrable as why there should be a buyer for everyone who seeks to sell. October 24 1929 showed that what is mysterious is not inevitable. Often there were no buyers, and only after wide vertical declines could anyone be induced to bid'.

Within 24 hours City bookshops had run out of copies of Galbraith's book.

Initially – because of the dislocation to business and financial activity caused by the storm – London was spared what New Yorkers, with their love of colourful euphemisms, called a 'meltdown' of share values. But by the evening of Monday October 19, now remembered as Black Monday, panic selling had swept through the City, and British share prices had fallen by one eighth. By the following night, Tuesday October 20, the FT 100–Share index had lost more than one-fifth of its value.

The fall might well have been greater had all those who wanted to sell managed to get through to their brokers. Switchboards were jammed, and there were accusations that many market-makers had left their phones off the hook, reluctant to trade even at the low prices to which they had marked down most stocks, for fear that these prices were nowhere near low enough.

No major company's shares escaped the crash. More than 39 million shares in British Petroleum, the nation's biggest corporation, changed hands, with the price at one stage falling to as low as 271 pence, compared with the 410 pence it had been only a few weeks before. For the Government, which had been heavily advertising BP shares on television, urging investors to 'be part of it', the fall had special poignancy. In parting with that portion of BP not previously privatized, it had just set the price at 330 pence, thereby ensuring that the final privatization would become not only a dismal flop but a major burden for the professional underwriters.

Tens of thousands of small investors saw their precious capital ravaged, and discovered that buying shares was no longer like stepping on an upwardly-mobile escalator.

In London the Chancellor of the Exchequer also urged investors to stay cool, describing the market panic as a 'grotesque over-reaction'. This was sound advice, but even as he spoke institutions the world over were unloading stock. In Hong Kong the Stock Exchange shut down for a week, and this extraordinary measure reverberated and led to a rout in the Asia-Pacific region, which felt the impact of the crash more than anywhere else. In Sydney share prices fell by a quarter. In Tokyo they fell by one-fifth.

The gloom was to last three months – by the end of 1988 most markets had shown a partial recovery, although only Tokyo managed to regain its pre-crash values within the year.

Yet by the turn of the decade markets world-wide were again at peak levels. Optimism had returned. But in London the crash, economic recession, and the over-indulgence of the late 80s had taken their toll, and many of the new alliances formed after Big Bang had ended in tears.

The worst casualties were some of the American banks. Having come in and bought old British family firms, thrown money at them, and then, as losses mounted imposed stringent controls, they then either emasculated them, closed them down, or sold them off. For instance Security Pacific, in the 80s the fifth largest American bank, developed international delusions of grandeur, and became victim of its own ambition. It acquired one of the finest old firms, Hoare Govett, but never managed to get the culture right. It also lost millions of pounds. The best people at Hoare Govett became disillusioned and left, some were encouraged to depart, and the firm struggled. It then decided that to operate a broking firm under the aegis of a bank was a mistake, so formed a new operating company, Security Pacific Alliance, to control its British and Australian equity operations with a 49 per cent share in a management buyout. The whole venture has cost the California bank over £50 million.

Citicorp and Chase Manhattan were other American banks that bulldozed their way in and blundered their way out, leaving a trail of mistakes and broken careers behind them. European adventurers, more cautious, were more successful, and most of their operations are still intact, such as the Union de Banques Suisse ownership of Phillips and Drew, and Swiss Banking Corporation's partnership with Savory Milln. The Japanese, who avoided acquisitions, appear to have been the most successful, building their businesses slowly with the long-term in mind.

The large investment institutions – companies like Legal and General, Prudential and the Scottish life assurance offices – have benefited most from Big Bang, being able to pick up and choose with whom they deal and to negotiate very low rates of commission. The smaller investor has been the loser, driven away from the markets despite the transient attractions of privatization.

Wall Street

Wall Street is the term used to describe the financial district of New York, and, like the City, it occupies only a small area of the business capital of the United States. Wall Street is in lower Manhattan, and the stock market grew up there in support of the merchants and bankers who, two centuries ago, established themselves on the tip of the island, when it was the pre-eminent business centre of America.

In those days Wall Street was the most important thoroughfare. Cargo ships were moored on the nearby East River, and the commodities they brought were traded in offices and warehouses on what become known as 'The Street'. As in London, everything in the area was destroyed by a Great Fire: the one in Wall Street occurred in 1835, and the damage stretched from the present site of City Hall to the Statue of Liberty.

The New York Stock Exchange was founded on its present site, the block bounded by Wall, Broad and New Streets and Exchange Place, although it has been rebuilt several times since the construction in 1864 of Renwick's $2 million marble-fronted wooden building, highlighted by eight lacquered columns and a rococo cornice.

The first New York Stock Exchange was more like a gentlemen's club than a business centre. There were 1,100 members, and its books and records were as closely guarded as those of a Masonic lodge. There was an honorary president, with few duties, and two salaried vice-presidents, but they had little to do except open and close trading at the morning and afternoon sessions.

The Exchange conducted its business by way of auctions, not dissimilar to those used by Sotheby's in the fine art market. Sellers would hand in their shares to the vice-president, who would guard them rather like a cloakroom attendant at a large hotel. They would be auctioned in blocks, and sold to the highest bidder. Inevitably, as with real estate auctions, some deals took place outside the room, usually in the street, and a number of sub-exchanges grew up, often handling specialist shares.

One of these grew into an exchange of its own, operating from another building in Lower Broad Street, where it was known as the Open Board, so called because access was available to anyone prepared to pay a $50 membership fee. Once inside there was no auction, no organization and no records were kept: buyers simply met potential sellers and dealt. The Open Board operated six days a week, and kept open as long as there were sufficient people about.

Out of this chaos developed the ticker, telegraph machines which simply listed the latest prices at which stocks were traded. As access to the ticker spread beyond Wall Street and New York itself to other American cities, other share trading exchanges grew up, using the ticker as a guide to prices.

This development was viewed with some alarm by the elders of the New York Stock Exchange. Although the ticker services generated more business, their activities were outside NYSE control, their prices were sometimes wrong, and they led to the proliferation of rival trading locations.

In 1885 they denied the reporters of ticker companies access to the floor of the exchange, and forced them to purchase the information. Within five years they had control of the ticker, and were able to insist on the Western Union telegraph company distributing it, making it available only to licensed brokerages and other approved buyers.

By this time business had grown to such a level that the auction system could not cope. What took its place was a sub-system of specialist auctions within the trading floor.

Legend has it that a broker called Boyd broke his leg and, finding hobbling around the floor on crutches difficult, remained at one post to trade his shares. After his leg had mended, he discovered that this mode of operation had become so profitable that he stuck with it, thus creating the specialist market-making system that still exists today.

I can find no evidence that this story is anything but apocryphal, but something like this happened, and provided the basis for present-day trading in New York. These days about one quarter of the membership of the New York Stock Exchange are specialist-market makers, operating in 66 units. These units operate as principals in the shares in which they specialize.

A broker buying or selling shares on behalf of a client in any of the over 2,000 issues listed on the New York Stock Exchange will go to one of the 22 trading posts. There he will approach market makers, rather as in London brokers used to seek out jobbers, and seek a price. The market-maker is obliged to be ready to buy and sell, and he has to balance his own books. If he is left with an oversupply or shortage of stock at the end of the day he has to hold it in his own account.

In theory the market-maker only changes his prices by notches: thus he is not supposed to react to any dramatic turn of events by radical shifts. In practice he is human, and will not want to pay over-the-odds for a share which is tumbling. Running for cover is not encouraged. On the other hand when large institutions trade very large blocks of shares, it is unreasonable to expect an individual to hold out against a hurricane. The New York Stock Exchange attempts to keep market-makers on track by policing price movements very carefully, and by encouraging competition.

This competition exists, of course, within the exchange, but also from rivals. One of these rivals operates in an almost identical fashion to today's London market, and is known as the over-the-counter market, so called because sharebrokers anywhere in the United States or elsewhere can buy or sell stock for customers who drop by. This market is run by NASDAQ, an acronym for National Association of Securities Dealers Automated Quotation System.

Anyone with a basic awareness of MS-DOS computers

can grasp the fundamentals within minutes, and become an accomplished operator after half a day's training.

The American Prototype

Whenever a dealer makes a market – in other words provides a quote for the purchase or sale of a stock – he enters it into his terminal, which is on line to a national data base, to which all market-makers subscribe. Securities dealers in over 6,000 offices have at their finger tips an exact, national, instantaneous wholesale price system, available in San Francisco, Chicago or Dallas at the same time as Wall Street. Indeed, it goes beyond that. There are over 8,500 quotation terminals outside the United States, most of them about 5,000, in Europe, and NASDAQ plans to extend this.

Members of NASDAQ may act either as principals or agents. The principal, or market-maker, bears a close resemblance to a broker, except that instead of leaning against a bench in a crowded exchange, he is usually in an air-conditioned suite surrounded by monitors, banks of command telephones, and girls whose language leaves something to be desired. At any time during the day, he may enter against the name of a company a price at which he is prepared to buy its stock, and a price at which he will sell it. From time to time, he will update his quote, and he will follow news developments closely over the Reuter Money Line service. He trusts and hopes his price will be competitive with other market-makers in NASDAQ, and confidently waits for a telephone call from a broker thirsting to buy.

The NASDAQ system is of benefit also to anyone else in the investment business, from brokers in San Antonio to the man on the stockbroker counter at the local Sears Roebuck department store, and to those in London who want instant information about the American market. There is nothing to stop individual investors subscribing, and NASDAQ already has over 100,000 hooked up, including brokers who are members of the London Stock Exchange. Those who pay a small subscription have access to the system through a dumb terminal and a black and white monitor. By using a word code on the terminal keyboard, they can obtain on the screen a representative 'bid' and a representative 'ask' price on the stock; for example, if dealers or market-makers have quoted bids on a particular stock of 40, 40.25, 40.50, 40.75, and 41, the representative bid would be 40.5. If those with a terminal wish to buy or sell – or if their customer so wishes – all they have to do it to phone their broker and seek a real quote, asking that it should be close to the representative figure on the screen, and stipulating, if they wish, how far from the figure they are prepared to trade.

NASDAQ has a more sophisticated, and more expensive, service for professional traders. In this case, having obtained a representative quote, a user may then seek actual quotes from the firms making the market in the stock. This is what would happen if an individual using the basic service were to phone in. The screen would display all those offering a quote, together with their names and telephone numbers, ranked in order of best price. The final barter then takes place over the telephone, and the new quote is inputted on the screen, with the computer updating the representative or average price.

All deals in securities that are traded regularly and in large volume – a list of about 3,000 stocks – must be reported within 90 seconds of the trade taking place. There are safeguards built into the NASDAQ system to attempt to prevent malpractice, and to seek to provide the investor with the same security that he had under the London jobbing system. Dealers must have a net capital of $25,000, or $2,500 for each security in which they are registered, whichever happens to be the greater. Once registered in a stock, a NASDAQ dealer must be prepared to buy or sell at any time, in much the same way as a jobber has been obliged to stand behind his price. There must be at least two market-makers for each stock quoted.

A market-maker whose spread – the difference between his 'buy' and 'sell' quotation – is more than double that of the representative or average spread, will be warned by the computer that his spread is excessive. The computer warning also finds its way into the directories of the National Association of Security Dealers, which will almost certainly call for an explanation, and may take disciplinary action.

Another safety measure is a provision in the NASDAQ

rules that when a member dealer buys on his own account and not on behalf of a client, he should do so at a price which is 'fair' in relation to the prices being made by the market-makers. The factors which should be taken into account by both members and disciplinary committees in determining the fairness of such deals are set out in the association's Rules of Fair Practice, and include the type of security and its availability in the market.

All members of NASDAQ must be members of the Securities Investor Protection Corporation, established by Congress in 1970; this means that those who buy and sell through the system have exactly the same protection as they would if they were dealing on the New York Stock Exchange. If an investor, or anyone else, feels he had been maltreated, or that there has been malpractice, the SIPC will contact the Association, which maintains a three-year computer file record of every price movement in a stock, and may trace the history of the stock second by second, identifying when changes took place, who initiated them, and what was the root cause. With such a complete audit trail, investigations are relatively easy to conduct.

NASDAQ, with over 4,000 companies listed on its system, averaging a daily turnover of 150 million, is the fourth largest stock market in the world.

SEAQ

For NASDAQ read SEAQ, and you have the British Stock Exchange Automated Quotations System.

SEAQ replaced the old system on October 27 1986. Market makers tap into the SEAQ system the prices at which they are willing to buy and sell the shares of those companies in which they are authorized to make a market. Most market makers are at their desks at eight in the morning to review the papers rather like a punter studying the form. Once a bid and offer price have been entered, the market maker is obliged to trade at that price, although of course he can alter his figures at any time in response to market conditions – in other words after he has seen what the opposition is doing.

The SEAQ system covers more than 3,500 securities, and is divided into three groups of stocks – alpha, beta, and gamma.

As the name implies alpha stocks are the most actively traded shares, and market-makers who buy or sell must immediately enter the trade into the SEAQ system. From SEAQ the trade details are passed instantly to TOPIC, the London Stock Exchange's electronic information service, which is available to traders, brokers and investors at varying levels of sophistication. Stock Exchange members authorized to trade get the complete picture – the range of quotes from all the market makers and the details of the last transaction in each stock. Other subscribers – investment institutions, private investors, journalists and basically anyone prepared to pay – get a trimmed down version which provides a single best quote for each SEAQ security held in the database, and, for alpha stocks, the number of trades in the previous five minutes and for the day as a whole.

So, to return to the example in Chapter One of the investor purchasing 500 shares in British Petroleum, how does the new system work? His broker or licenced financial intermediary SEAQ will call out the BP page from the system, and see an array of offers from more than a dozen market-makers, each of them identified by a code. One line will say 'HGVA 36–40 1 × 1'. This means that Hoare Govett, for example, are prepared to buy BP at £5.36 and to sell at £5.40, and that their figure applies for purchases or sales of 1,000 shares or less. Another line might say BZW 36–41 1 × 2', indicating that Barclays De Zoete Wedd will buy at the same price as Hoare Govett, but that they will only sell BP at £5.41, and then only in units of up to 2,000.

Another page on SEAQ will reveal that ten minutes earlier there had been a large transaction of BP shares at £5.38. Assuming he wants to trade, the broker calls the dealing desk of his own or another firm and asks to buy BP at £5.40. If the broker's firm is also listed as a market-maker in BP, the broker will try and keep the deal 'in-house' by persuading his own colleagues to match the Hoare Govett offer, which they may or may not be willing to do. When the bargain is struck, the market-maker enters it into the BP SEAQ page; other market-makers, noting the transaction, readjust their offers accordingly.

Deals in beta stocks are concluded in exactly the same way, except that not all trades are logged, and there are fewer market-makers, perhaps only two or three, who will usually be firms that have decided to specialize in a particular sector, such as electronics, or insurance. At the time of writing the London Stock Exchange was planning to reduce the number of beta market-makers to one. This would be a retrograde step, eliminating competition and increasing investors' costs. In the case of gamma stocks, only indicative quotes are provided, so that any broker anxious to consider a purchase has to call the market-maker and negotiate a price, often based on volume. Many of the market-makers in the gamma section may be regional brokers, who know companies in their area well and are better placed to hold the book than a large London conglomerate.

The new system removes completely the disadvantages once suffered by regional stockbrokers. Not only may they act as market-makers in regional stocks, but they have the same instant access to pricing enjoyed by those whose offices are in London or New York, and will no longer be obliged to deal only as agents. The new system is also capable of accommodating many more members, who may live in a different time zone altogether, such as Hong Kong or Bahrain, although such firms would have the added burden of having to meet the laws in their own countries as well as the strict rules of the London Stock Exchange. But it is probable that some offshore centres will accept the British regulations as their own, and therefore offer the prospect of substantial new markets for securities traded through SEAQ.

One danger seen in the new system is that, because there is no longer a strictly independent intermediary, the jobber, who lived or died by judging the market price correctly, brokers can in theory sell to each other at prices which might bear little relation to the market, thereby feathering their own nests. Furthermore, if the market-maker has taken on a bad stock and made a loss on it, one of his dealers could attempt to unload it on an unsuspecting investor. If this happened on a small scale, there would be a few aggrieved investors who presumably would never deal with the firm again. If it happened on a large scale, there would be a major outcry. Such practices, of course, are strictly proscribed by the rules, and in the United States the powerful Securities and Exchange Commission maintains a close watch on share dealings.

Through SEAQ, the Stock Exchange is confident that such crooked practices will be detected and wiped out, and the Stock Exchange's own surveillance unit maintains a close watch on unusual pricing and share movements, monitored by a very powerful computer programme. Under the new Stock Exchange rules, where no market-maker is involved, reporting must be done by the broker executing a deal reporting by telephone or telex to the Exchange, where the trade will be entered into the SEAQ system for the purpose of surveillance. So even if the unwary client has not realized that he has been charged too much for a particular stock, there is a fair chance that the 26 inspectors at the Stock Exchange will have spotted that the price paid is out of line. If the client himself believes that he is the victim of a scam, all he has to do is to inform the Exchange of the exact time the deal was struck, which will be recorded on all future contract notes. The Exchange will replay the relevant SEAQ database (all tapes will be kept for five years) and will immediately be able to spot whether the price was a genuine error or the result of sharp practice. A tracer is also put on the deal, and any related transactions. It was this system that spotted unusual movements that led to the downfall of a leading executive of Morgan Grenfell in November 1986.

For the technically-minded, the SEAQ system operates on two dedicated mainframe computers, designed to respond to entries within one second, update information at a peak rate of 20 items per second, and handle up to 70,000 transactions an hour. This is more than twice the 1984 total market volume of trades. In the event of a computer crash, a major fire or bomb outrage at the Stock Exchange, all the records would be saved, for parallel computers operate in another part of London and, for double protection, in the United States. The entire capitalist system is not likely to fail because of a power cut!

Brokers and dealers get their information through an IBM-PC, or compatible equivalent, connected to the SEAQ system either by direct data line or, in the case of the smaller user or provincial broker, by a leased telephone line. Those who wish to use the system only occasionally may do so through an ordinary phone line, connecting their computer to the jack via a standard modem. Those on the move may use a laptop computer plugged into the telephone.

4 Nomura Makes Money Make Money

On a busy day the stockmarket in Tokyo resembles a surging crowd at the Kop end of Anfield, the home of Liverpool football club. The dealers face the various display boards, indicating the latest prices, and at the slightest sign of action or excitement, surge forward together, their hands outstretched in unison in a kind of salute for capitalism. In mid-1991 Tokyo had a market valued at over $2,800 billion, and, on average, 500 million shares change hands every day.

Since World War II it has overtaken all the other exchanges in its volume of share trading, and is second only to New York in the value of stock moved. But for all this strength it is an erratic market, relatively open to manipulation. From time to time it also runs short of liquidity. The Tokyo Stock Exchange is unlike any other exchange in its mode of trading, because it combines the specialist system of New York with electronic trading. The shares of Japan's major corporations, and some overseas multinationals, are traded in what is called the First Section: dealing is broken up into a number of key industry groups, such as electronics, chemicals, utilities and so on.

In 1990, there were 1,200 corporate stocks listed in the First Section with a market capitalization of 404 trillion yen. The Second Section comprises smaller companies, and although some trading does take place on the floor, much of it is done through computers by a system known as CATS, Computer Assisted Trading System.

Dealing is handled by member brokers, including a number of overseas securities houses. Getting a licence in Japan is both expensive and time-consuming; the licences have only been made available to non-Japanese under substantial pressure from the United States and Europe. In the Pacific rim, Tokyo has become by far the most important financial centre, surpassing Hong Kong, whose reputation suffered not so much as a result of fears about the future at the expiry of the New Territory leases but from a series of financial scandals resulting in the prosecution and ultimate imprisonment of its chairman.

Tokyo's international role was not planned. It was a by-product of the Japanese government's decision to liberalize the financial sector, mainly for domestic reasons. Japan is now the largest exporter of capital in the world. The main source of this flow of yen outside the country is the huge pool of money saved by Japanese men and women. They save almost one-fifth of their incomes each year, putting money aside at four times the rate of Americans. This prudence generates roughly $3,500 billion a year. Another factor is the Japanese trade surplus created by successful exports. Although some of this money has found its way into industrial investment – such as Nissan's successful car assembly plant in the north of England – much of it is invested in equities and bonds in the United States, Europe and Australia.

Another way this pool of wealth may be tapped is by securing a listing in Tokyo, so that Japanese may invest in your corporation without moving their money outside the yen zone. But, unlike London, Tokyo has so far not promoted itself vigorously as a financial centre. One reason for this is that if it did so the Japanese government would find itself exposed to criticism that it was seeking to keep its financial surpluses at home. Much of this criticism is ill-founded, because if that was the case, then the yen would rise to such a point that exports would not be maintained. But despite this lack of promotion more and more international companies have been seeking to list their shares in Japan, despite the expense of doing so. Though costs vary, a multinational is unlikely to be able to get a listing through for less than $100,000, plus $75,000 a year running expenses.

Many companies do so in the hope of attracting Japanese shareholders to their registers. But I think a more compelling reason is that a listing ensures that the Japanese investment community, at all levels, gets to know about them, thereby providing immediate recognition and some long-term commercial benefits. Conducting business in Japan can be a complex and frustrating experience. A listing on the Tokyo Stock Exchange automatically bestows a Japanese status on foreign companies, making it easier for them to deal with both local and central government in Japan, Japanese industrialists and consumers.

Take, for example, Britain's leading trading bank and financial institution, Barclays. It has had representation in Japan for more than 20 years, was the first European bank to obtain privileged Japanese trust bank status, and decided it should list because, as the bank's Humphrey Norrington put it to me: 'We are a global business, and therefore want to reflect that in the ownership of our shares. Secondly we have quite a big business in Japan, and we want to be able to use this share ownership as a way of increasing our picture, and we want to increase the number of owners of our shares'.

The reasoning was put the other way round by a senior staffer at Nomura Securities: 'The Japanese do not buy unfamiliar companies unless it's an exciting stock'. He said he thought a Tokyo listing useful for 'any company that has a consumer orientation and has identification at a retail level, and any company that has major operations in Japan or Asia. Heavy borrowers should also consider a TSE listing. If you've got all three it's a must'.

However obtaining and maintaining a listing in Japan carries with it considerably more work than achieving the same position in London or elsewhere. Applicants must be prepared for rigorous investigation by Japanese regulators. Once accepted, good investor relations become another substantial commitment. There is also another worry – the technical problem known in the jargon of stockbroking as flowback. What happens is that if an investor in a company listed in London or New York cannot buy sufficient stock in those markets, he may simply instruct a Tokyo broker to purchase it in Japan. Thus the Tokyo equity may end up being largely held, not by Japanese or Asian investors, but by Americans or Europeans, thus defeating the whole purpose of a Japanese listing.

It is inevitable, along with the shift of world economic power from the Atlantic to the Pacific, that the Tokyo Stock Exchange will gain in both stature and size. Its members work long hours in a vigorous market. Ten years ago

Japanese fund managers and market experts had a reputation for having no imagination and showing excessive caution. This is seldom the case today. 'We are stock-picking on an international scale – we intend to be number one', the senior manager of one of Nomura Securities' divisions told me.

Over half the business in Tokyo is handled by just four firms – Nomura, Yamaichi, Nikko and Daiwa. The big four account for three-quarters of all underwriting business in Japan, and half of all share broking. Nomura Securities is the world's largest securities house. Founded as a small money-changing shop in the back-streets of Osaka in 1872, it now makes more money than Japan's two auto giants, Honda and Toyota.

In Japan it wields enormous power. Every Tuesday afternoon, at its headquarters in the Urbannet Otemachi Building, its senior stock-picker issues its selection. Nomura salesmen on the fifth floor telephone the prized information to selected clients and to the firm's extensive branch network, and within minutes the Tokyo stockmarket in Kabuto-cho is scrambling with buying orders. Nomura has sales shops right across Japan, mostly staffed by women who visit clients door-to-door, and who sell aggressively on the telephone. This network was built on an old idea, adopted from the 'Man from the Pru' in Britain. The Japanese version has Nomura representatives lending wooden savings boxes to housewives, asking them to put all their 10-yen coins into a box.

Nomura provides a good example of Japanese aggression conducted with dignity and a certain amount of stealth. From its unpretentious headquarters in Tokyo it spreads its tentacles across every continent with offices in 28 cities in 19 countries. Its market capitalization is US$ 60 billion, and it has 15,000 employees. It is by far the world's largest and richest securities house, earning more profits than Barclay's Bank and J. P. Morgan combined. In 1986 it chose London as the location of one of two world regional centres – the other is in New York – and its declared aim is to become the dominant financial institution in every area of business. It is clear that, together with its domestic rivals, Daiwa, Nikko and Yamaichi, it poses as great a threat to the City as Sony and NEC have been in the electronics industry, and

Toyota, Nissan and Honda to the motor industry. It will succeed by ruthlessly cutting prices to gain market shares – it has already done this in the bond markets. In London it has bought the vast old General Post Office building in St Martin's Le-Grand, and has preserved the façade while gutting the interior to provide one of London's most impressive headquarters buildings. This is the Japanese technique – to operate behind the shelter of a local façade in just the same way that Nissan used a British company, Datsun UK, to build up a presence.

It seems improbable that Nomura will, in the short term, buy a British bank, like Midland or Lloyds, but more likely that it will be a wholesaler of finance and financial products, perhaps using a building society network at one end of the scale, and a sophisticated investment bank dealing with mergers and acquisitions at the other.

In recent years Nomura has been the largest single employer of Oxbridge graduates, ousting Unilever, BP, Shell and ICI from the top spots. These new recruits are each year flown to Tokyo for six months' training, and quickly become enthusiastic about their new employer.

'I joined Nomura because I think their global expansion programme is absolutely phenomenal', said Christopher. 'I am sure they are going to come up as number one ahead of the others'.

'They are going to be very, very big', said Catherine. 'They are very ambitious, and the togetherness and the spirit really is obvious'.

'They really believe in team work', said James, 'yet I am also amazed at the degree of responsibility that last year's graduates have been given'.

Didn't any of these young Britons feel uneasy that their country's own institutions might suffer as a result of the sheer force of Nomura's thrust? All scoffed at the suggestion. James held up a white Nomura carrier bag.

'I joined a Japanese institution for precisely that reason', he said. 'I have brought this to show you because it sums up Nomura's attitude. It says: 'Nomura makes money make money'. Now a British institution would probably have had a Latin ode. Nomura knows what it is up to'.

5 Europe

When, in the winter of 1990, the Berlin wall came crashing down, symbolizing the end of the Cold War, there was an atmosphere of unrestrained euphoria. Germany, at last, could be reunited. New democracies in Czechoslovakia, Hungary, and Poland would take their rightful place in the European Community.

In February I was staying in a small pension in a ski resort in Switzerland when a fleet of black cars turned up bearing Chancellor Helmut Kohl of Germany and the leaders of these emergent countries. Over lunch they talked bravely of the new dawn, how together they would help to rebuild Europe from the Atlantic to the Urals. At the World Economic Forum in nearby Davos they were besieged by businessmen anxious to take advantage of the new opportunities in the East.

One year later, at the 1991 Forum, the atmosphere was totally different. The faces of the East European government leaders showed the strains of office. There was not enough money to rebuild their shattered economies, production was falling, and unemployment was rising above 25 per cent. Vaclav Klaus, Czechoslovakia's finance minister, told me: 'Things could not be worse'. Chancellor Kohl was suffering politically because of the financial strain of supporting the East. Lester Thurow, dean of the Sloan School of Management at the Massachusetts Institute of Technology, said: 'What Europe needs is a Marshall Plan. If something is not done you will have a migration problem: the Poles will be in Paris'.

Having abandoned communism and embraced capitalism, the 'ossies', as they were called, found that the system that had bought riches to the Germans, the French, the Dutch and the Italians appeared incapable of doing anything for them. The saner amongst them realized, of course, that the wrongs of 50 years could not be put right in five minutes.

But capitalism was showing its cracks, and the biggest disappointment was that Europe's share markets failed to rise to the occasion. The buccaneering spirit that had seen the rise of Britain's first two public companies, the Muscovy Company and the East India Company, was not alive on Europe's bourses.

The cost of rebuilding the East will be about one trillion dollars – and there are only three ways in which it can be found. The first is by taxing those who will benefit by an expanded market – West Europeans. This is political suicide. The second is through bank loans, but the banking system in the early 90s was already overstretched. That leaves the bourses, which in Europe lack leadership and cohesion.

With the exception of London, which, in any case has a global rather than a European vision, the bourses in Europe have traditionally been narrow institutions, focused in the past, with little vision beyond the national boundaries of the countries in which they operate.

One reason for this, of course, is that they were shattered by the Nazi domination of Europe in World War II, when capital in many countries was devalued or destroyed. But that does not wholly explain their relatively insignificant role in capital formation. The real reason is the dominance of banks, both as a vehicle for individual savings and a source of finance for industry.

As Anthony Sampson explained in his book *The New Europeans*:

The big continental banks evoke a much deeper dread than the British, partly because they have embraced industry with a closer hug. Their power goes back to the nineteenth century. The French Rothschilds helped to finance the railways in France and beyond, and their rivals the Pereires set a pattern for the 'universal bank', collecting savings from small-savers and deploying the capital for the development and control of industry, which was followed elsewhere in the continent. The French banks soon fell behind the German banks, who played a key part in the new industries, and used their deposits, and their customers' proxies, to establish controlling shares in the big companies. A German bank, as the saying went, accompanied an industrial enterprise from the cradle to the grave, from establishment to liquidation throughout all the vicissitudes of its existence.

Even a writer with Sampson's capacity for thoroughness could find no room for the bourses in his 450 pages. This is not surprising, given their insignificance as Pan-European institutions, and the lack of a truly European stock exchange.

So when compared with the big three – London, New York and Tokyo – the other markets are relatively small. The combined market capitalization of all the European exchanges is little more than half that of London. The largest, Frankfurt, which like Paris has pretensions to challenge the British capital for financial centre supremacy in Europe, is not much more than one-tenth of the value, with 743 companies listed compared with 2,559 in London.

But change is in the air. The single market in Europe in 1993 is supposed to lead to a common capital market, and if the grip of state-controlled telecoms utilities can be broken then there is no reason why share markets should not operate together, linked by cable, satellite and computer. There are 325 million people living in the European Community of 12 member-countries, and there is no logical reason why they should not be able to access any of the capital markets through national bourses or mini-bourses established in every town. Buying stocks should be as easy as obtaining foreign exchange.

Much work needs to be done to fulfil these high expectations, and the first step in this direction is expected to be a European list comprising between 200 and 300 European blue chip companies and government bonds quoted simultaneously on all stock exchanges in the community. An information network called PIPE, an acronym for Price Information Project Europe, is under development.

But as Dr Gernot Ernst, the chairman of the Federation of German Stock Exchanges, said in his 1989 annual report: 'Care should be taken not to fight yesterday's battles . . . thinking in terms of professional grouping and regional market share is inappropriate in an age where we are rapidly approaching the de facto globalization of the financial markets'.

Yet the German markets have a public relations battle to persuade the corporate sector to make more use of outside financing as distinct from internally-generated funds. And, as Dr Ernst put it: 'A number of things have to be done in Germany in order for its financial markets to gain the importance that is commensurate with the role of the Deutsche Mark and the German economy. There is perhaps sometimes a lack of courage to call traditions into question, and if necessary to throw things overboard that have become outdated'.

The principal change needed is to unlock institutional cash for the equity markets. At present institutional interest is meagre. Insurance companies, the mainstay of the markets in many countries, have just five per cent of their assets in shares. Pension funds, amounting to some DM 300 billion, are reinvested in the balance sheets of their own companies, due to German tax incentives to keep them there. This huge flow of internal capital means that large German corporations do not often need outside capital.

At the official level the Bonn government is helping by abolishing stock exchange turnover tax, a quarter of one per cent each time an equity is bought or sold.

There are eight stock exchanges in Germany but Frankfurt, with a trading floor of 6,500 square metres plus state-of-the-art technology, is by far the most significant. The Deutscher Aktienindex – known as the DAX – is the most widely quoted barometer of German stocks, based on the prices of the 30 most-heavily traded shares and updated every minute of the trading day. The more broadly-based FAZ index contains all the German shares officially listed on the exchange.

Additionally there is KISS (Kurs Information Service System) which captures and transmits in real time the prices for all shares traded in Frankfurt, as well as providing some of the Paris Bourse prices, and business and economic news. These prices are relayed instantly to news agencies, which publicize them world-wide. Frankfurt is also the only exchange in Europe which has a live television programme, *Teleborse*, broadcast direct from the trading floor.

If Frankfurt still has much to do, mainland Europe's second largest exchange, the Paris Bourse, has radically transformed itself in recent years. Its fine historical building on Rue de la Bourse belies the fact that, operationally, France now has one of the most modern and efficient stock exchanges in the world, with both screen and floor trading, a modern transactions system, known as Relit, and deregulated commissions for brokers. But it is still perceived to be over-regulated by the French government.

The six million Swiss are perhaps the most heavily banked people on earth, and until recently had seven stock exchanges upon which to trade shares. But the Big Three banks – Union de Banque Suisse, Swiss Banking Corporation and Credit Suisse – decided to put a stop to this, and withdrew their support from the four smallest. In the end Switzerland may well end up with only the Zurich bourse, controlled by the banks. In Zurich there are no market-makers and no brokers: virtually all the work is done by the bankers' representatives, who only abolished fixed commissions because the Swiss Cartel Office forced them to do so. Institutional investors are not particularly active: Swiss pensions funds, with $150 billion under management, have only about five per cent in local equities, though this is expected to increase. Despite its strong role as a banking centre, Zurich is not an important bourse. The 12 major Swiss stocks are also traded in London on SEAQ International, which handles a fifth of total Swiss trading volume.

Eastern Europe

The video produced to celebrate the reopening of the Budapest Stock Exchange laid bare the wishful thinking of those pushing through economic reforms in Hungary. There were the usual images: dealers shouting at each other, their telephones wedged between ear and shoulder, one hand scribbling, the other operating a keyboard. Young women stared pensively at their screens; other swivelled in their chairs and scowled in a questioning manner at colleagues. The video showed the global markets in action: New York, Tokyo, London, Frankfurt, and, of course, Budapest.

Of course the Budapest Stock Exchange is not like that. Its venue – the baroque banking hall of the Bank of Budapest in Vorosmarty Square – owes more to the polished charm of the Austro-Hungarian empire than to the contemporary dealing room. The trading room has polished marble pillars and brown panelled walls, not false ceilings and smoked glass. But for the new paint and the gilded brass chandeliers, dangling incongruously over a bank of computers, it might have been the old exchange closed by the Communists in 1948 and now exhumed from a time warp.

Trading is not exactly brisk, more a trifle forlorn, although there is the promise of more activity as privatization gathers apace. But when the exchange reopened, on Midsummer's Day 1990, after a 42–year break for the communist experiment, only three companies were listed. These were Ibusz, the Hungarian travel agency; Novotrade, a software house, and Skala, the country's largest cooperative retailer. In addition there is a market in some 400 corporate bonds, traded by bankers' representatives.

One of the first international visitors to this limp, fledgling market was then British Prime Minister, Margaret Thatcher. She congratulated Lajos Bokros, president of the exchange and a former communist, on being 'ahead of Moscow'. He replied that 'small is beautiful' and from tiny acorns great oaks are born.

Be that as it may, it will be a long while before stock markets in the former eastern bloc attain any size of strength. Very few easterners have substantial savings – or are prepared to admit to having them. Surplus funds have traditionally been kept under the mattress or in attics. Western investors are unlikely to use the Budapest market when most Hungarian companies of any substance are listed in Vienna. You can also invest in Hungary without going anywhere near Budapest. The large American securities house, Merrill Lynch, has launched an Austro-Hungary fund, which is denominated in dollars and listed on the Amsterdam bourse. In 1990 the Bank of Hungary had $3 billion of Eurobonds out in the market, most of them denominated in German marks. Some funds had raised large amounts of cash to invest in Hungary, but had found difficulties in finding suitable opportunities. The First Hungary Fund, launched by Bear Sterns and Co, raised $80 million, while the John Govett-run Hungarian Investment Company raised $100 million, but by the end of 1990 neither had made an investment in the country.

6 The Share Buyers

'When Stocks goes down, shoeshines go down. It's rough — Wall Street Shoe cleaner.

'Have I made thee more profits than other princes can' — Prospero in The Tempest, Act 1, Scene II.

'Millions of the new investors have never traded a share, nor do they know how to do so. They only own one or two shares bought in the generously priced and heavily marketed privatisation issues. They tend to see share ownership rather as a sophisticated gamble than as a long-term investment in the wealth-creating process' — Sir Peter Thompson, chairman of the CBI Wider Share Ownership Council.

Screen trading and deals by telephone have removed much of the lively atmosphere that used to be part of the daily life of stock exchanges. In London, for instance, where there is no longer a trading floor, there is little of interest to the casual visitor. But where exchanges still operate with an open-shout system, you will usually find 30 or 40 onlookers, most of them middle-aged. Some scan the boards with binoculars; others seem mesmerized by their own thoughts.

Most people who hold shares will never visit a stock exchange. They call their broker, and leave the rest to him. In America, where large national broking firms have branch offices in most towns, it is common for the private investor to drop by, look at the television screens bearing prices, and enjoy a cup of coffee and a chat with the local manager. It becomes a social occasion. Such share shops exist in shopping malls and in department stores like Sears Roebuck. Japan has investment shops in every town.

In Europe it is different. Investors prefer to conduct their business more discreetly, a throwback perhaps to higher personal taxation. On the Continent there is a tendency to favour fixed-interest securities. Even in Britain the number of people who actually own shares is not rising significantly.

One of the objectives of the Conservative Government in the Thatcher years was to turn Britain into a nation of shareholders. As an objective it was commendable. Individuals would be able to benefit from prosperity and economic growth, and would feel they had a stake in the country.

The instrument for carrying out this objective was privatization: the disposal of public assets for cash. Instead of the government holding all the shares in public corporations like British Gas, British Telecom or electric power generation and distribution, individuals were invited to become shareholders, and provided with valuable incentives to do so.

It was – and is – a sound idea. It was a policy which was picked up and followed throughout the world, particularly in Eastern Europe once the new democracies broke away from the influence of the Soviet Union. Even the Kremlin, pursuing President Mikhail Gorbachev's policy of perestroika, has been seeking to introduce it.

Unfortunately, however, the way privatizations have been carried out in Britain has left much to be desired. The chief beneficiaries have been, not members of the British public, but the large institutions, domestic and international, who were given preferential treatment. Others who were benefited were intermediaries such as merchant banks, large legal and accountancy firms, and public relations firms.

By the turn of the decade the great privatization sales led to one in four families in Britain owning shares. But almost two-thirds of the 11.5 million shareholders held equity in only one company. The company tended to be the one they worked for, or British Telecom or British Gas. These small portfolio gains for private owners were dwarfed by the money pulled out of the share markets by individual investors. More than £3 billion has been withdrawn from the equity markets by private individuals in each of recent years. By contrast in socially-mind Sweden 46 per cent hold equities.

Betting shops have proliferated while share shops foundered. Sir Peter Thompson, chairman of the Confederation of British Industry's Wider Share Ownership Task Force complained: 'Millions of the new investors have never traded a share, nor do they know how. They only own one of two shares bought in the generously priced and heavily marketed privatisation issues. They tend to see share ownership rather as a sophisticated gamble than a long-term investment in the wealth creating process.'

Could we ever return to the days when the private investor held a higher proportion of the British market? If individuals are to increase their stake from 20 per cent to, say, 30 per cent, over the next ten years, they will have to invest at least £9 billion. This seems improbable, and it would require a change in savings habits by average families. The British save more than £50 billion each year, but the lion's share goes into building societies and banks, as well as pension schemes and life assurance policies. Many of these are compulsory, and so money could not automatically be diverted into private equity plans even if the will was there to do so.

If the private investors' place in the market was considerably larger, the balance would be better. As the London Stock Exchange's Andrew Hugh Smith put it, there would be a diverse body of investors 'with different time scales to the institutional manager, with different investment objectives in general, and a greater willingness to move in the opposite direction to the herd.'

This would be a highly desirable scenario in any country, but it would not be achieved by mere numbers. Most private shareholders are traditionally passive. The classic case is of Aunt Maud, who inherited a handsome portfolio of shares from her father, and who will pass them on to her nephew in due course. In the meantime she takes little interest in the performance of her shares, and keeps the certificates, like a piece of valuable but unworn jewellery, in a bank vault.

What is needed is not the creation of tens of thousands more passive owners like Aunt Maud, but people who buy shares with the desire to pay attention to their investments. But that will require changes of policy and practice by the Government, as well as a new attitude towards small investors in the City of London.

One of the most important changes needed would be to reduce the expectation that an investment in property is to put a family on the road to riches. Many of those who

bought a home in 1989 would perhaps argue that this point
has already been achieved, in view of the fall in house prices
at the turn of the decade. But that was a phenomenon rare
in Britain. On the whole the two-thirds of the British population that live in their own homes have enjoyed untaxed
capital gains well in excess of any taxable profit likely from
the equity market, and so have committed increasing sums
to property. Were the government to tilt the scales by making
equity ownership more attractive while removing some of
the tax breaks available to home owners, the amount of
money available for share investment might rise substantially. The most important of these tax breaks is the relief
given on mortgage interest and the absence of a capital gains
tax on owner-occupied property.

Apart from home ownership, the income return on a
deposit in a building society looks attractive to many people,
mainly because they perceive it as an investment totally without risk. This is probably because few of the investors understand the concept of total return – in other words evaluation
of capital gains as well as dividends when assessing earnings.

But even if the Government adopted none of these measures, the financial services industry could do much to promote
private share ownership. Many of those in the City of
London have an antipathy towards private investors from
the middle or working classes. Financial services institutions
have conducted major advertising campaigns to persuade
those who have bought shares through privatization to trade
them in for collective investments like unit trusts, which, of
course bear high management charges which have to be paid
by the unit holders. Many of these funds are not particularly
well managed, and traditionally perform less well than the
Financial Times-Stock Exchange 100 Share Index.

One of the most unpleasant features of the institutional
fund management attitude towards private shareholders is
their 'mother-knows-best' attitude: indeed their campaigns
have a familiar ring about them; that of Labour governments
in the fifties and sixties who believed that they, rather than
the taxpayer, knew how best their money should be spent.
An example of this City arrogance occurred at the time
of electricity privatization, when the BBC provided a free
platform to one of the City's lively marketeers, in which

he argued that most individuals were not suited to share ownership, and that their money was better invested in collective schemes. Like those run by him, of course.

But distaste for dealing with those wearing boiler suits rather than those with pin-stripes is not the only problem. Many of the large share-broking firms claim that they cannot afford to handle transactions by private individuals involving sums under £5,000. This is true, but it is because of their high overheads and other costs, rather than for the technical reasons, such as settlement procedures, usually put forward.

Of course ordinary families do not normally deal in the City. After all, if you wish to pay your phone or credit card bill you go to your local bank or building society, not to a merchant bank. You may, of course, buy shares through a branch bank or building society. Most of the larger organizations have subsidiaries which provide a share dealing service. One of them, Barclayshare, makes it easy, providing several levels of service according to customers' requirements, as well as a place for certificates to be lodged, regular portfolio valuations, and an annual statement of dividends for the taxman. But, with this exception, none of the share-dealing services are well advertised, and the impression remains that the branch manager would rather sell you a life assurance policy or a personal loan.

The lowest cost solution for the private individual who wishes to conduct part of his or her investment through equities is to join a service like Barclayshare. A trade can be executed just as quickly through this system as through any London private broker. The investor has the choice of either discussing his portfolio with an investment manager – and paying for that service – or acting on intuition. If the latter is the choice, then it would pay to become a regular subscriber to an intelligent weekly publication such as *The Economist* or the *Investors Chronicle*. The serious Sunday newspapers also all provide a useful service.

Those small investors who feel they would prefer something more personal than a service offered by a bank may obtain a list of stockbrokers prepared to deal with small clients from the Stock Exchange in London. Seekers of a 'dealing only' service should concentrate on the percentage commission and the minimum commission. It is likely to start at 1.5 per cent for small deals, but with a minimum charge of £20. Those who require a regular supply of investment advice and analysis will have to pay substantially more, unless they are frequent traders in reasonably large blocks of stock. Then they will be offered additional services, such as the ability to buy nominee stock. Then there is portfolio management, for those prepared to entrust £50,000 or more to the broking firm to handle at its discretion. Apart from paying commission, the investor may also have to pay an annual fee. If the fee is high enough brokers may rebate all or part of the commission. In many cases it is better to pay a fee so as to avoid the incentive that commission-remuneration provides to brokers to churn stock.

But the sad fact is that in Britain most people invest in the share markets indirectly – through the large institutions. These may be life assurance companies, investing the premiums that are placed with them, or pension funds, operated for large corporations or private individuals. Or they may be mutual funds or unit trusts, running collective investments for those who wish to see their savings spread among a number of equities or fixed interest securities.

Nowhere has this trend towards collective investment been more marked than in Britain. Here the percentage of the British stock market controlled by private investors has fallen from 28.2 per cent in 1981 to less than 20 per cent in 1991. Thirty years earlier, two-thirds of the stock market was in private hands.

Whereas the political catch-cry of privatization across the world was that it would disperse wealth across the social spectrum – particularly allowing workers to take a stake in the enterprises by whom they were employed – in practice control of corporations is increasingly concentrated in fewer hands. Ownership and control by the state has been replaced by domination by fund managers.

Most fund managers have never scuffed their hands in manufacturing industry, or hustled for business in an overseas market, or designed a robot, a machine tool, or a new building. Whether based in London, New York, Tokyo or a handful of other financial centres, they wear grey pin-strip suits and the introverted look of someone who has spent too long staring at spreadsheets and annual reports.

Because they can sack boards, determine the outcome of takeover bids, and make or break corporations, they are lobbied by a new breed of public relations consultant: the investor relations specialist, who, in turn, is hired by corporate managers keen to keep their jobs intact. Gone is the Victorian-style capitalist, the owner-manager accountable only to himself.

In Britain just ten men control one quarter of the national economy, operating funds with a total worth of £100 billion. Whether it is right or proper, in a democratic country like Britain, for a small group of individuals to control such a large proportion of the nation's wealth is very questionable. In his book *Rule Britannia*, my friend James Bellini argues that the power of the City institutions has led to the decline of industry and increasing speculation in land and services.

Table 1 Britain's largest shareholders

Name	Equities managed in $ billions
Prudential	18.0
Mercury	15.0
Kuwait Inv.	11.0
Postel	10.0
Flemings	8.5
Standard Life	7.5
BZW Inv Man.	7.5
Norwich Union	7.3
Schroder	7.2
Phillips/Drew	7.0

Source: *Phillips & Drew.*

The institutions take themselves, and their jobs, seriously. Hardly a working day goes by when they are not meeting with directors or managers of companies in which they have invested. Although they deny they have a day-to-day influence on managers, they do step in and exert their power when things go wrong.

Whether in Europe or elsewhere, institutional investors differ in their objectives according to the sector in which they are.

Pension funds – by far the most important in size of assets

invested – invest the contributions of employees and their employers with the objective of maximum gain, so that the obligations of their various schemes may be fully and easily met. They are not above a bit of speculation, but generally their funds are directed towards meeting the pledges made to employees without necessitating an increase in employers' contributions. The better a pension fund is managed, the lower the employer's cost. So most pension funds, including those run exclusively for the benefit of trade union members, allocate their investments across a broad spectrum, preferring a diversified portfolio, as the jargon puts it, to excessive concentration in one or two stocks, or venturing into risky projects. Almost all pension funds have, in recent years, also diversified their portfolios to include investments in the United States, Western Europe, and the Far East and Pacific Basin.

Life Assurance Companies

Then there are life assurance companies, whose principal concern is to ensure that the premium incomes received are invested adequately to meet the eventual pay-out upon death or the end of a term. It is necessary for these hugh investors to match their known obligations, calculated through actuarial tables, with investments maturing at the same time. For this reason assurance companies invest heavily in long-dated gilt-edged securities or bonds.

Some governments insist that institutions like life assurance companies and pension funds, which are often the recipients of generous tax treatment, allocate a substantial proportion of their investments to gilt-edged securities or semi-government bonds. There is, however, a trend away from such rules. Australia, for instance, abolished what was known as the 20/30 rule whereby for every $30 invested elsewhere, $20 had to be invested in government bonds. Japan, whose pension funds have colossal clout, has gradually been easing the restrictions which made it difficult for large sums of money to be invested elsewhere than in Japanese industry.

The absence of regulation does not stop critics of capitalism objecting strongly to privileged institutional investors failing, in their view, to use their funds in the national interest. Present Labour Party policy in Britain is that pension funds should be obliged to invest much of their money in British industry. The counter-argument, of course, is that it is the duty of pension funds and life assurance companies to do the best they can for those whose money they hold in trust – future pensioners and policy-holders – and therefore their fund managers should be unfettered by nationalistic controls.

Both arguments have been well aired, and in the second half of the 1970s a Committee of Inquiry headed by the former Prime Minister, Harold Wilson, investigated the matter thoroughly, while also focusing specifically on the charge that lack of controls had denied British industry or would-be entrepreneurs adequate capital. In its report, published in June 1980, the Committee resoundingly rejected the charges, and to this day no solid evidence has been produced that worthwhile ventures are denied funds. If anything, the margin of error has been the other way: the City and institutional investors have been only too willing to rescue lost causes that should have been allowed to pass into liquidation or more competent hands.

Unit Trusts

The other set of powerful institutional investors are mutual funds, known in Britain as unit trusts, and investment trusts, and other managed funds. Trusts provide ways in which small and medium-sized investors can take an interest in equity markets without having to take the risk of buying shares in individual companies.

There are over 1,200 unit trust funds in Britain alone, managed by 154 separate London groups. Some of the groups are very large; the Save and Prosper Group, for instance, employs 700 people. As a glance through the advertisements in the Saturday papers show, there is a unit trust for everybody: trusts that offer the prospect of capital gain, and those that offer income; trusts that invest in blue-chip stocks, and those that specialize in high-risk, or 'recovery', stocks. There are now even trusts for those who will only invest in ethical propositions. These eschew stakes in tobacco companies for instance. Almost all unit trust management companies, many of them owned by banks, merchant banks, or insurance companies, have specialist country funds. The most popular are those with portfolios in Western Europe, the United States, Japan and Australia, and the more stable countries of South East Asia – in other words stable economies. There are, as far as I know, no unit trusts offering units in Chile, Zimbabwe, or the Soviet bloc, although that may come.

A good idea of the range available can be seen by looking at the funds managed by just one average group, Montague Investment Management, headquartered in London. MIM Britannia Unit Trust Managers operates 40 trusts. Four of them are British specialist funds, seven are general funds, five are bond-related high income trusts, and the remainder are divided into sectors or countries. The specialist funds cover such fields as commodity stocks, gold, financial securities, property and international leisure. International funds are confined to Europe, North America and the Asia Pacific region, but cover small companies and recovery units as well as general equities and bonds.

Most unit trust managers also offer life or pension-linked funds, which in Britain allow the investor substantial tax advantages, in that the cost of units is permitted as a tax deduction so long as the investor does not sell the units or receive any dividends until retirement age.

Another form of unit trust investment which has become popular because of its tax efficiency is the umbrella fund, which allows investors to switch units between funds, without being liable for capital gains tax on any profit on the deal. This allows both fund managers and private investors to operate efficiently in the widely fluctuating foreign exchange markets; anyone moving in and out of American dollar equities at the right time during 1990 and 1991, for instance, would have enjoyed a substantial capital gain.

Although, in common with equities, unit trusts performed badly in the mid-1970s, they have produced adequate returns ever since. Indeed, except for those with homes in the southeast of England, they have offered a better return than real estate. Someone with a house in Liverpool, say, would have done better to have sold his house upon retirement ten years ago, invested the fund in unit trusts, and rented a villa in the Algarve or Majorca.

On the other hand, over a short period, investment in unit trusts can lose money. On August 1, 1988 all 100 unit trusts in the UK general sector had lost money over a one year period – this, of course, taking into account the October 1987 crash. The average fall for the year to July 30 1988 was 22.4 per cent, compared with a decline in the Financial Times All Share Index of 19.7 per cent. But over the period of five years to May 1991 they gained 51 per cent.

One of the problems with unit trusts, from an investor's point of view, is that it costs rather too much to buy them. There is usually an up-front charge of 5 per cent, plus the burden of VAT, so that quite often it may be some time before the buyer can see any improvement in his portfolio. The spread between the bid and the offer price is also often large – 6 per cent or more, with some as high at 14 per cent – so your units will have to rise appreciably before you can sell them at profit. And the more you switch the more it costs, which may help the intermediary or discretionary portfolio adviser, but is no use to the investor at all.

There are also widespread differences in the performances of the various funds, a fact which seems to escape much public notice.

The first May issue of *Financial Adviser* in 1991 showed that over the previous 12 months, the Bishopsgate PEP unit trust had outperformed everyone – £1,000 invested in it would have risen to £1,360. On the other hand £1,000 put into MGM's special situation fund would have been worth only £560. Of course these tables are about as useful as a league table in professional football. Just because you are top one month does not mean you will stay there. But just as Liverpool FC is usually to be found in the top six of British Football clubs, so the best funds show a consistency. Before making any unit trust investment it would be sensible to study the tables in publications like *Financial Adviser* or *Money Management* to check performance levels.

Investment Trusts

Often confused with unit trusts, but different in concept, are investment trusts. Like unit trusts, investment trusts allow the smaller private investor to benefit from having a stake in a large portfolio of widely spread shares, both by sector and by region. But there the similarity ends. Investment trusts are public companies like any other public company, and their shares are traded on the Stock Exchange; instead of making motor cars, running hotels, or operating department stores, an investment trust company exists purely and simply to buy and sell shares in other companies, both for short-term speculative gain and long-term capital growth. Those who manage investment trusts, full-time executives responsible to a board of directors, buy and sell shares on the world's stock exchanges, exercising their judgement as to what will be a profitable investment. Just like any other public company, they make profits and incur losses, and pay dividends to shareholders. Because their companies have assets, investment trust executives can borrow against those assets, and are able to take both a long- and a short-term view of the money entrusted to them. Capital gains on share trading are not distributed in cash but used to build up portfolios and, through the kindness of the Chancellor of the Exchequer, escape taxation. Investment trusts have about £20 billion under management with 250,000 investors.

Investment trusts are cheaper to invest in than unit trusts. As stated earlier, for every £1,000 invested in unit trusts, it costs £50 in an initial management charge. The same amount used to purchase shares in an investment trust would incur less than £30 in stockbroker's commission and government stamp duty. Unit trust managers also charge an annual fee of between 0.75 to 1.0 per cent for looking after their trusts; investment trust management charges are much lower.

So why do average investors not flock to investment trusts? The answer is hype. Unit trusts are prolific advertisers in the financial press, and therefore get much more than their fair share of space in the editorial columns. By contrast, investment trusts are restricted by law in their advertising, and get comparatively little press attention. The serious newspapers provide free space to unit trusts to publicize their prices, acknowledging it a public service to do so, but provide only limited price information on investment trusts.

Moreover unit trusts are, like most life assurance products, sold by middle-men – insurance brokers, financial advisers, even accountants and solicitors. They received a handsome commission from this form of activity, most of it up front. With the exception of investment trust savings schemes, there is no commission for intermediaries on investment trusts, so, for the most part, they do not recommend them. This, of course, makes a nonsense of the idea that the average insurance broker is a genuine financial adviser. Investment trusts deserve a place in everyone's savings portfolio, and, in many cases, offer a better return than the average with-profits policy.

Another important difference, seldom understood, between investment trusts and unit trusts is that the latter are priced according to their net asset value. Investment trusts, like other equities, are valued according to what the market thinks they are worth, which is more often than not below the value of their assets. This is partly because it is recognized that disposing of assets costs real money, but it also reflects the market's perception of the business and the economic environment. The result is that something can be built into an investment trust's share price for future prospects. This can never happen for a unit trust.

There are now nearly 30,000 investors in Britain using investment trusts, accounting for over £20 billion. It is surprising the figure is not higher.

Managed Funds

The final group of large institutional investors is different again. These are professional fund management groups, which manage, at their own discretion, the money of others, both individuals and companies. Here again there are similarities with previous groups.

At one end of the scale, there are large stockbroking companies, which take in funds from individuals who either cannot be bothered or feel they lack the expertise to watch the market. These individuals, which range from pensioners in Worthing or Westchester County to wealthy Arabs in Dubai, entrust sums of money – the minimum is usually at least £10,000 – to fund managers within broking houses who manage their portfolio, and keep them posted, through a quarterly or half yearly report, as to what they have done with it. Only rarely would a fund manager consult a client about the purchase or sale of an investment, though most of them are receptive to suggestions. Many broking firms' fund management teams invest in unit trusts and investment trusts, and some have portfolios that stipulate such a limitation.

Some broking houses charge for this service; others rely for income on the commission obtained through sale and purchase of shares, or from a percentage paid to them by unit trusts. This itself can lead to conflict of interest. Those brokers that leave an investment undisturbed are obviously going to benefit less than those that are constantly trading their customer's portfolio, and on many occasions there is much to be said for sticking with the status quo.

At the other end of the scale are the large fund management groups, often a major branch or department of a well-known merchant bank. The principle is the same as with small portfolio management by brokers, but their clients are usually foreign potentates, and other very large clients for whom they also act as investment bankers.

The funds under their stewardship are usually measured in billions. For instance, in 1985 Baring Brothers and Co. Ltd managed funds of more than £2,500m., just over half of it in Britain, with clients as diverse as Bowater Corporation, London Transport and London University. More than twice as large, in fund management terms, is Robert Fleming Investment Management Ltd, with £5,800m. of clients' money to invest, including some of the funds of the Royal National Lifeboat Institution, IBM, Dow Chemical, and Whitbread. Recently Flemings have pushed hard with some success to manage the vast pool of money in the Japanese pension funds.

Other big fund managers include GT Management, with the BBC as a client, Hambros Investment Management, Hill Samuel, Lazard Securities, Montague Investment Management, UBS., Phillips and Drew, J. Henry Schroder Wagg and

Co., N. M. Rothschild Asset Management Ltd, and Warburg Investment Management.

For all of these groups fund management means a lot more than sitting in a City office, reading research reports, and studying the prices on the electronic monitors. The good fund manager needs to have the judgement of Solomon, the speed of decision-making of a track bookmaker, an ability to size up a balance sheet in minutes, the nose for news of a good newspaper editor, and an eye on the main chance.

With intense competition, both to sell and to perform, and round-the-world trading, the active fund manager can only grow old in the job if he or she is prepared to put work above everything. It is a long way from the days when the investment manager of the Pru' would make his way back to his office from a lunch at the club to place an investment of £1m. in the British Motor Corporation.

The Fund of Funds

Late 1985 brought the development – the fund of funds, designed to minimize risk for the small investor and to remove him one further stage away from direct purchases of shares. Instead of having to pick and choose between 800 unit trusts, the investor could buy units in a master fund, which in turn would buy units in one or more of its subsidiary funds. From the point of view of someone with a small amount of capital to invest – but no clear idea if and when to move out of a British equity trust and into a Japanese, German or American one – the fund of funds seems no bad idea. Let someone else do the worrying and save yourself the expense of having a stockbroker to manage a portfolio of unit trusts.

Like most bright ideas, the notion was not a new one. The fund of funds first obtained notoriety as a promotion in 1962 of the international investment swindler Bernie Cornfeld, whose misdeeds are well spelt out in a brilliant book *Do You Sincerely Want To Be Rich?* by Charles Raw, Bruce Page and Godfrey Hodgson. This cautionary tale should be required reading for both investors and all those involved in the financial services industry. As the authors say:

The salesman's rationale for the Fund of Funds was an unusually owlish piece of nonsense – one of those things that sounds impressive until you really think it through. Mutual funds, and all investment concerns, are sold on the proposition that the ordinary man needs investment advisers to make choices for him. The Fund of Funds went further and suggested that the ordinary man now needed professionals to choose the professionals who would make the choices. The Fund of Funds would take your money, and invest it in other mutual funds – but only in those whose values were rising most rapidly.

A lawyer from the US Securities and Exchange Commission exploded the Fund of Funds argument succinctly:

> If funds of funds are permitted to proliferate, how would an investor decide among the many companies seeking his investment dollar? Would he not need a fund of funds of funds to make this decision?

Cornfeld's Fund of Funds run by his Investors Overseas Services and given the hard-sell by thousands of salesmen calling themselves 'financial counsellors', gathered in $100m. of people's savings within two years of its launch. The customer's money was transferred immediately into separate proprietary funds, for a brokerage fee which was pocketed by IOS. For the privilege of investing at all, the customer had to pay what has become known as a 'front-end load', much of which was used to pay a commission to the salesman who persuaded him to part with his money in the first pace. For every $3,000 invested in Cornfeld's Fund of Funds, $540 vanished immediately in fees. A further 10 per cent of any income generated also went in fees, as did 10 per cent of any capital gain. According to Raw, Page and Hodgson an investor had to wait six years before he could even get his money out without loss. An investigation found that money which was supposed to be held on trust for customers was being used for the benefit of IOS itself, its directors, employees and friends; and that the IOS sales force engaged in illegal currency transactions on a major scale, and constantly misrepresented the investment performance of its largest fund.

Whitehall Relaxes the Rules

The shockwaves that surrounded the fall of IOS were such that the Department of Trade and Industry put a stop on the establishment of any other funds of funds. So adamant were the men in Whitehall that the concept was fraught with danger that few financial institutions bothered to apply for approval of schemes they preferred to call 'managed funds'.

But there were good arguments in favour of them. A fund of funds saves small investors from the perils of switching. It also saves a small problem over capital gains, for an investor transferring from one unit trust to another and making sufficient profit in the process could be liable for capital gains, even though he is only being prudent in transferring an investment to a different sector. A fund of funds is not liable for capital gains.

But strict rules were introduced. An approved fund of funds is restricted in its investments to its manager's own unit trusts, in total contrast with the United States where master funds may invest in anything but their own in-house trusts. A new fund of funds must also be in a group holding at least four subsidiary trusts and not more than 50 per cent of assets can be invested in any one of them. It is allowed to make an initial charge to investors, but cannot charge unit holders a further front-end load when buying into a subsidiary fund. It may also charge double annual management fees.

Despite these rules there are problems. The most serious of these is conflict of interest.

If the manager of a fund of funds is not to upset his colleagues running one of the subsidiary unit trusts in which he must invest, he will have to avoid sudden switching, particularly of very large sums. But if he is not prepared to move in and out of the subsidiary funds as and when he sees fit, he will miss the market opportunities available to those who manage individual portfolios.

Despite these reservations, the fund of funds concept seems here to stay. And if such funds grow in popularity, they have plenty of scope for expansion at the expense of the building societies. One building society alone, the Halifax, controls more than the entire unit trust industry.

Funds of funds are also likely to be taken up by the life

assurance industry. Ever since the Government ceased to allow life assurance or endowment premiums as a tax deduction, removing from life assurance companies a substantial privilege, the flock of commission-remunerated salesmen who have made a living from selling life assurance have had little to sell. Such is the awareness now of the public to the range of more attractive alternative investments available that cold canvassers from the life assurance industry calling on engaged couples or distressed widows have found their job extremely difficult.

Stockbrokers like John Savage of Hoarde Govett believe the life assurance industry needs to be quick to grasp the fund of funds concept. 'There are a lot of intermediaries who really cannot any longer sell their products on investment grounds, and they need a new package to sell. I do not believe these products have been produced to be sold directly to the public. They have been produced for the professional intermediary who has not got a clue about what is going on in the investment world. He is good at selling something. It might be double glazing, it might be insurance bonds, it might be unit trusts, but he has to have a product to sell, and one that will be easily sold on the basis that the client he is selling to won't ask the right questions.'

Paperchase

'There is a discrepancy in London between the efficacy of the trading system and the efficiency of settlement operations. Some back offices are still in the Victorian age' – Annual report of the Frankfurt Stock Exchange, 1989.

Buying and selling shares is a brief transaction, often no more than two phone calls. But, unlike the housewife purchasing a kilo of apples from a market stall, the sharebuyer has nothing physically to show for it, other than a debit on his bank account after he has written out a cheque to his stockbroker. In order to be able to sell his shares again at a later date, he or she requires proof of ownership.

Traditionally this has been the share certificate, a legal document issued by the registrar of the company that issued the shares in the first place. With millions of shares changing hands each day – many of them in large blocks – settlement has been a cumbersome paperchase, employing thousands of people and costing investors, companies, and brokers millions of dollars to operate.

When London had a trading floor the details of all transactions recorded in the broker's dealing book were entered in ledgers, or computer programs, back at the office. The client was sent a contract note and a share registration form, which he had to return, together with an account. In London there were 22 accounting periods during the year, and statements were normally sent out after each one. Anyone who bought and sold their shares during an accounting period – a short-term speculator, for instance – would not have to pay for them.

The jobber's dealing record was also committed to ledgers back in his office, and it was here that the paper chain began. If he had bought shares in the market, say 1,000 ICI, he would expect to be able to find someone to take them over before the end of the account period, relieving him of the necessity to chase up the scrip. In the example where he sold 500 BP shares, things might have been more difficult. Within the accounting period he would expect to come across a seller of BP shares, hopefully prepared to sell at less than he had sold the earlier lot for, to enable him to cover his position and to make a profit.

But where he was a seller of shares, he faced the task of producing the scrip; in other words, to ensure that the share certificates were passed to the broker acting for the purchaser. With small parcels this was relatively easy, but where large trades occur, he might incur some difficulty. In any event it was unlikely that he would be able to match the sale exactly, so to obtain the scrip for any one parcel sold, he might have to go to several sellers for shares, thereby necessitating several contract notes to complete the transaction.

Back in the broker's office, clerks had to enter details of all these transactions into several other ledgers. There was the client ledger, dealing with each customer's transactions, which formed the basis of client billing. There was a list book, classified under the names of shares, to keep track of all trades. Each day clerks from broking houses would meet in the settlement room at the Stock Exchange to check the bargains reported by their dealers. Sometimes, in the mêlée of a busy day, errors occurred. Where the error was not the obvious fault of any one party, losses would be divided.

Once clients buying shares had returned their registration documents and settled their accounts, the broker had to make sure the relevant share certificates were provided to them. Share certificates were delivered by the selling brokers to the Central Stock Payment Office of the Stock Exchange, sorted into correct destinations, and collected by messengers of the buying brokers. For the reason explained earlier, in many cases there was more than one certificate, often from more than one individual. In the case of someone buying 1,000 ICI shares, for example, the certificates would come in odd lots, perhaps from different parts of the country. Details of the names and addresses of the former owners of the certificates would have to be recorded in yet another ledger, before the certificates were scrutinized by clerks for authenticity, and then sent off, together with the transfer authority, to the share registry of the company concerned. Very few listed companies, whether large or small, maintain their own share registry, preferring to pay for the services of specialist registrars, often operated by bank departments scattered around the country. Lloyd's Bank's Registry department at Goring-on-Sea is one such registrar, and has become one of the largest employers in West Sussex; during the height of the British Telecom flotation it was handling more than one million pieces of mail a day.

The system had barely changed for two centuries, and by 1980 it had become costly and grindingly slow. With up to half a million tickets and transfer forms passing round the market at the end of each account period, it was often many weeks before the purchaser of shares received the evidence of his purchase, by which time he might well have sold them again. It was costing registrars £75m. a year to maintain the share registers for just 9,000 securities.

Then the London Stock Exchange introduced the Talisman system. The definition of the Talisman system given in its brochure speaks for itself.

'*Talisman, tal'is-man, or-iz-n. Transfer Accounting Lodge-
ment for Investors, Stock Management for jobbers: Gr. payment, certificate, later completion; or an object induced with
magical powers through which extraordinary results are
achieved.*'

Given the cumbersome nature of the old system, it was
not surprising that the Stock Exchange waxed lyrical about
Talisman; anything which can cut out such a complicated
paperchase would be credited with magical powers. Yet the
theory behind Talisman is very simple.

Under Talisman the title of each share changing hands is
transferred from its registered owner to Sepon Ltd, which is
a Stock Exchange nominee company formed to hold shares
in trust on behalf of the underlying new owner, whose
interests are at all times fully protected. Sepon Ltd then
transfers the shares on to the buying client.

It works like this. When the selling broker receives the
share certificate and the returned signed transfer form from
his client, he deposits them at the nearest Talisman centre,
either in London or at one of eight other centres located in
major British cities. At the Talisman centre the documents
are checked for accuracy, and the transfer information – the
names and addresses of the sellers and the contract price –
entered into the central computer system. This is based in
the Stock Exchange building in London on two computers,
with the entire system being periodically operated at another
site in Britain.

The documents are then passed from the Talisman centre
to the company's registrar for registration out of the client's
name and into that of Sepon Ltd, although control of the
stock remains with the selling client until payment is made
and delivery effected. When that happens ownership is transferred within the Talisman computer to the buying jobber's
– or market-maker's – account. Individual items of stock
lose their identity, and simply become a pool of shares with
which to satisfy buyers. The buying broker simply calls up
Talisman and the purchase information is entered into the
computer, which generates bought transfers, authorizing the
removal of shares from the Sepon account into the name of
the buying client. These bought transfers are sent on to the

registrar, who transfers registration out of Sepon, and posts off a new share certificate to the purchaser.

The Talisman system also generates accounts for over 200 member firms of the Stock Exchange located in 65 cities and towns. By belonging to the network, each firm has only to write (or bank) one cheque in each accounting period. The system acts as a clearing-house between all the member firms, apportioning debits and credits, and providing them with a detailed statement, which they use to check their own records. Talisman also calculates payments due to the Inland Revenue for stamp duty, pays them regularly in bulk, and debits brokers' accounts.

The system has important benefits for investors, especially over matters such as dividends, bonus issues and rights issues, which often become payable either just before or immediately after a sale of shares. The legal date for entitlement to dividends and such issues is the date of registration, and because Talisman has speeded up the registration process, annoying disputes can be avoided. Dividends received by Sepon Ltd are passed immediately to the entitled party.

Talisman is also used to settle international trades, providing benefits to those who deal through members or affiliates of the Stock Exchange. South African registered securities may be settled through the system; indeed for those investing in South African stocks it provides by far the swiftest way of doing so, and well before the end of the decade similar links will have been created with the other major share trading centres.

The Bull Brings Taurus

While Talisman was a major advance over the cumbersome old systems, it was not efficient enough to cope with the surge of action that accompanied the 1987 bull market and subsequent crash. A backlog built up of nearly $17 billion worth of unsettled deals. For eighteen months, the back offices of London's sharebroking firms were inundated with paper. Settlements that had been achieved swiftly under the old system were taking weeks, even months, as those in settlement departments tried to cope with the rush. Many firms introduced compulsory overtime over weekends, and some staffs also worked until late in the evening in an attempt to catch up.

This – and the evolution of international, all-electronic trading – led the International Stock Exchange to set up a task force to monitor each member firm's progress. The upshot was that the ISE decided it would have to reduce, even abolish, paper share certificates. So it announced its intention to launch a computerized share directory, in which transfer of shares would take place simply by moving the shares from the seller's directory in the computer to the buyer's. The directory was to be known as TAURUS, which stands for Transfer and Automated Registration of Uncertified Stock.

It is planned that TAURUS will stand behind TALISMAN, which will remain the means by which share transactions are reported, confirmed and settled. Details reported by TALISMAN will be entered into the TAURUS network by firms of brokers given the status of account controllers, who will also have the obligation of reporting ownership changes to company registrars. The system removes the need for paper certificates, though private shareholders will almost certainly seek a record of their holdings.

This proposed system has attracted widespread criticism, and its proposed introduction in 1989 has been repeatedly delayed. The argument in favour of having existing broking houses act as controllers is that it saves the cost of maintaining a separate central share register, a bureaucracy which some would rather avoid. But, mindful of City of London scandals and the collapse of a number of broking firms, sceptics have been asking what protection will be available to investors if brokers default when they have shares in their charge. Company law in Britain also has to be changed to transfer to a computer proof of ownership previously furnished by a share certificate.

What is likely to happen in the end is that a small number of banks and leading securities houses will act as custodians for share owners, rather as Barclayshare will do for private individuals today. The custodians may or may not be the investor's broker, and will be paid a standard fee for keeping the electronic records. According to the level of trust between the custodian and the investor, the custodian will issue some form of legal document proclaiming that it is the holder of a certain number of shares in certain companies for the benefit of the investor. What this means, in essence, is that the custodian will act rather like the nominee holder of shares.

Options and Futures

'If you are very good at market timing, you can make out like a bandit', said Donald Mesler of Chicago, author of *Stock Market Options*.

Options
For those prepared to risk a little money on speculation, options offer an attractive prospect. Many people have been heard to say: 'I would like to be able to buy shares in BP, ICI, or Hanson Trust, but their prices are so high I could not possibly afford them.' Leaving aside the loose logic of that statement – for an individual can always buy 50 or even 25 shares if he wishes – it is true that the chances of a major capital gain on one of the large and better known shares are slim.

That is, unless the investor wishes to try options. For example, let us say that on 19 December an individual thinks that Marks and Spencer is going to achieve record Christmas sales and that the margins will be such as to generate handsome profits for the company in the current financial year. He fancies chancing about £1,000 on his belief that the shares will rise. But at a notional 175p. each £1,000 will buy him only about 570 shares. If, in the months ahead, the share price rises to 190p. our friend will have made a capital gain of £85.50, less two lots of brokerage charges plus Value Added Tax. On options he would have done much better. His £1,000 would have bought him almost 7,700 3–month call options at a cost of 13p. each – the premium quoted on 19 December. This gives him the right to buy those 7,700 shares at any time in the next three months, at the 19 December price of 175p. When the shares rise to 190p., therefore, he will have made a capital gain of £1,155 – in other words a return in excess of 110 per cent on his original investment. He will not even have to find the money to pay for them, provided he buys and sells within the same Stock Exchange accounting period. However, should the shares fall over the three-month period by 15p. each, he will either have to find the full cost of 7,700 shares – in this example it would be about £13,500 – or forfeit the option to buy, which means that his £1,000 outlay has been lost.

If the stock is one in which the Stock Exchange runs a traded options market, then the investor has another possibility open to him, and that is to sell the option to another investor. The price of a traded option is decided by two factors: the underlying price of the share itself, and the market's expectations as to which way it will move in the weeks or months ahead. Obviously those operating in the traded options market expect to make a profit, so there is a premium to be paid for selling the unexpired portion of an option rather than sitting it out. But where an investor playing fears he has made a major misjudgement he can, to some extent, cover a big position by using the traded options market.

Another form of option is the 'put' option, which is the opposite of a 'call' option. A put option is taken out in anticipation of a fall in the value of the relevant share, and gives the owner the option to sell a quantity of shares at a given price.

It seems that in Britain the concept of investing in options has not caught on among general investors, although it plays a major part in the lives of the professionals. In the United States, where attitudes are rather different, options are booming. The Chicago Board Options Exchange is the second largest securities market in the United States, behind only the New York Exchange. The US regulatory authorities are also strong supporters of options trading, with the Securities and Exchange Commission arguing that it significantly enhances liquidity. But if you imagine that by buying options you are sure to win a fortune, be warned by the following remark from Stephen Figlewski, the Associate Professor of Finance at New York University:

Small investors lose because they believe their information is better than it really is. They take positions that aren't any better than their beliefs, and their beliefs aren't any better than throwing darts.

Futures

If trading in options sounds a little like a casino, it is dull by comparison with the activities on the futures markets. There are futures in everything – commodities like cocoa, coffee, wheat, lead, zinc and gold; meats like cattle and pork; currencies like the dollar, the yen, the German Mark, and the pound; and of course, shares.

Buying futures is speculation, and some people make and lose millions by doing it. It requires knowledge of changing circumstances, as well as intuition as to the way events will turn out. If you think that there will be a severe frost in Brazil – or are prepared to bet that this will be so – you may buy 6–month coffee futures, in the belief that by the time your coffee is delivered at the end of the period, it will be worth a lot more. Of course, there is no need for you to take delivery of the coffee at all; if the frost comes, the price of your futures contract will rise sharply, and you may sell out.

There is, of course, good reason for buying futures other than speculation. If you are a coffee wholesaler and you fear a cold snap in Brazil, you will buy futures to protect yourself, regarding the extra cost of the contract as an insurance premium. The same is true of the manufacturing industry. If you have ordered an expensive set of machine tools from Germany, due to be delivered in six months' time, you will not want to pay for them until delivery. But supposing the pound falls against the Mark in the meantime? You cover yourself by buying the required amount of Deutschemark futures. This process is called 'hedging'.

There are futures markets in all the major financial centres, while Chicago has assumed pre-eminence in the trading of commodities. London was slow to see the potential of futures markets, but in September 1982, members of the Stock Exchange joined forces with banks and commodities brokers to establish LIFFE – the London International Financial Futures Exchange – in the Royal Exchange building adjacent to the Bank of England and close to the site of the famous old coffee houses. LIFFE futures and options contracts have the great advantage of being 'exchange traded', and so are claimed to be free of credit risk, while their prices are displayed worldwide. When LIFFE was opened it was hailed as an institution that could maintain London's place at the heart of the world's financial system and divert business from the United States, denting Chicago's supremacy. By mid-1988, LIFFE was putting through 60,000 contracts a day, with most of the action concentrated in the Eurodollar, sterling, and gilt-edged contracts.

The biggest growth in turnover is likely to be in the gilts and interest-rate contracts, for the increase in the number of gilt-edged market-makers has placed a premium on hedging contracts. For instance, a fund manager may know that in three months he will receive cash for investment in gilts, and he has picked long gilts – those maturing in 15 years' time. Rather than waiting to see what the interest rate will be at that time, he can lock into today's rate by buying LIFFE's long gilts futures contracts for delivery in three months' time. If gilt yields then decline, the investor will have to pay a higher price, but the price of the long gilts futures contracts will have risen, and the fund manager's profits will reduce the effective cost of buying the stock.

The FT-SE 100 futures contract is priced by taking one-tenth of the value of the FT-SE 100 Share Index published throughout each business day. It may be used by an investment manager concerned that the market will rise before he can place funds becoming available to him.

7. What About the Workers?

'The capitalist gets rich, not, like the miser, in proportion to his personal labour and restricted consumption, but at the same rate he squeezes out labour-power from others, and compels the worker to renounce all the enjoyments of life' – Karl Marx.

Political parties of all persuasions throughout the industrialized world now agree on the need for those who work in an enterprise to share in its profits. In most Western countries the drive for the workers to have a say in the way the company for which he works is run – a process known in Europe as co-determination – has been largely overtaken by a push for workers to own shares.

It is not easy to determine what led to this change of emphasis, or whether it is a change that is permanent. It could be a short-term phenomenon, built on the rising prices of shares in most companies throughout the long bull markets of the 80s. Or it could be through the need to increase savings, and what better way to achieve this than by encouraging people to invest in their own enterprise and endeavour?

From Warsaw to Washington workers now own shares, but there is a considerable debate on the effectiveness of employee ownership. So far there is little evidence to suggest that employees use their position as shareholders to influence boards, although in some cases workers have delegated their voting rights to trade unions. Even in companies where generous workers' participation exists, their collective holding seldom rises above five per cent. There is also an argument that workers should behave in exactly the same way as prudent investment managers, and spread a share portfolio over a number of stocks to minimize risk. Certainly an *employee* with shares in his employer should be wide awake to the downside possibilities – in other words that he may lose all or most of his investment.

Another complication comes when employee share ownership is mistakenly seen as a form of performance-related pay. Share ownership is not, and should not, be seen as an alternative to incentives. Share ownership gives employees a stake in the capital of a company, regardless of whether individually or collectively they have made a positive contribution. Profit-related pay and bonus schemes, which may be based on meeting budget or on the return of capital, however desirable, are quite separate.

Nevertheless those concerns that have introduced generous schemes to enable employees to own shares believe attitudes have changed. One such firm is the PA Consulting Group, with employees in 20 countries owning shares. Roger Cadman, the personnel director, says it has created a more commercial outlook. 'The whole aggregate of the million little decisions and actions that people take has an effect'.

Fabled ESOPS

ESOPS stands for employee share ownership plans. They were first introduced in the United States, and now exist in Britain and other countries as well. Essentially companies borrow funds from banks to buy shares for distribution among the workforce, with the interest charges being wholly or partly tax deductible.

In 1989 and 1990 bank lending to ESOPS in the United States was almost $US 50 billion, with the cost to the taxpayer working out at about $US 2.5 billion. There are approximately 10,000 American companies running ESOPS, covering 10 million employee shareholders.

In Britain ESOPS were slow to catch on. One reason was the legal requirement for an approved scheme to reward all employees equally. Some companies preferred to limit plans to management, and introduced share option schemes instead. But the development of ESOPS was mostly inhibited by the law which forbade companies from giving financial assistance for the purchase of its own shares. This particular rule was changed in the 1990 Budget to allow ESOPS schemes to be funded, and it remains to be seen how successful they become.

Privatization: Privileges for the Workers

Few employees have fared so well as those working for privatized concerns in Britain, for in almost all cases they were offered privileged treatment both on price and allocations.

Let us look at just one example: the employees of Northumbrian Water, the most over-subscribed of the ten new water companies. Those who did not live in Northumbria were restricted to just 100 shares each, and even the customers were allocated only 200: hardly worth the bother, and almost a waste of time. Those who worked for the company, however, had every reason to smile, for they were entitled to apply for and get up to 5,000 shares. Workers at the other companies received the same preferential treatment.

The Northumbrian shares were priced at 240 pence, payable in instalments, but water employees were able to invest at a 10 per cent discount. When trading started on the share-markets, the opening price showed a premium of 60 pence a share. A worker taking his full allocation would have shown a paper profit of about 84p per share.

The water workers – along with other employees of privatized concerns – have also enjoyed other special privileges denied to others, the most significant of which is exemption from the punitive taxation imposed on their counterparts who work for other companies seeking extra capital through rights issues. Although companies offering rights issues normally allocate employees shares – through the distribution of the so-called pink forms signifying a priority offer – those workers who take advantage of this have to pay tax as PAYE on the premium to the issue price when the share starts trading, as if it was income. Indeed so unfair is this rule that most employees end up having this tax deducted from their wages before they are able to dispose of the shares. The workers of privatized companies face no such intolerable burden.

The 90,000 workers of British Gas were also given generous treatment, which cost the taxpayer a total of £54 million. Each employee was awarded £70 worth of shares, plus a further £2 worth for each year of service. Those able to invest their own money were given two free shares for each one bought, up to a limit of £300 of free shares. Those inclined to dig deeper into their savings could buy up to £2,000 worth at a ten per cent discount. Pensioners were also each given about £75 worth of free shares. This was in sharp contrast to the parsimony of British Telecom, whose employee shareholders missed out.

In all the major privatizations so far, the majority of employees have taken up their entitlements, though many later sold or reduced their holdings. Foolishly perhaps, most employees sold their holdings on the market, rather than to work colleagues or trades unions, for had they adopted this latter course they could have wielded more influence in their companies. To some extent this happened in the case of British Airways where 5,000 employees gave their union a proxy vote over their shares.

Since the BT days many unions have decided to take a more pragmatic line towards share ownership. For example, the eight unions in the Electricity Supply Trades Union Council claim that they are still vehemently opposed to privatization of Britain's power industry, but in early 1990 were accepting that they could do little to stop it and were hard at work trying to negotiate a more generous handout. As John Lyons, general secretary of the Engineers' and Managers' Association put it: 'We have to deal with practicalities. Members will be given shares, and it is our job to get them the best deal possible'. Another trade unionist, Jim Mowatt, of the leftish Transport and General Workers' Union, added: 'People do have ideological objections, but you have to confront reality, and the reality is that workers want shares'.

8   Raising Money

Almost every entrepreneur has a dream that he will be able to build up his own business as a private company, and then, because of its success and opportunity for further growth, be able to sell it to the market. For many the happiest solution is to find large numbers of individuals prepared to buy a total stake, of say, 47 per cent, so that the original founder and his family may retain control, while pocketing the cash generated by the sale. The lucky few who do this become instant multi-millionaires, and are still able to hold on to the businesses they started and to run them in much the same way as before.

So how can an entrepreneur use the stock markets for his own benefit? The cardinal rule is that there should be some other reason for turning a private company into a listed one rather than just to obtain a personal fortune. It would not be easy to bring a company to the markets if that were seen by the markets as the prime purpose.

The most obvious attraction of going public is that obtaining a listing on any major stock exchange improves the standing of the concern and its products. There are very few manufacturers of branded products or household names that are not public companies or corporations.

Apart from obtaining a better image, becoming listed on a stock exchange also makes it easier, in normal times, to raise finance for expansion and development. Both investors and lenders have a distinct preference for an enterprise that is not the plaything of an individual, or a group of individuals. Even though it is still possible for one man to hold the reins of a large public company, there are many more checks and balances than on private companies, where clever accountants can play interesting games with the balance sheet. The accounts, and other indicators of performance, of public companies are closely scrutinized by meticulous analysts, who are ever ready to publish adverse comment where they believe it to be merited. Thus most public companies are assessed with one objective – are they good investments? Checking the potential of private companies is not easy, even when they are open to scrutiny; private company accounts are freely available only at Companies' House, and then usually one year in arrears. This alone explains why both institutional and private investors are reluctant to commit large sums to unquoted companies. What happens when the leading figures in a private company die? Their heirs may be hopeless businessmen, or may be forced to sell up part of their holding at an inopportune time in order to pay capital transfer tax. Father may drop dead just as the next recession is approaching: subsequent family feuding and a forced sale could leave the outside investors with little to show for their years of support to the old concern.

Another strong advantage to an expanding business in being publicly listed on an exchange is that it helps in takeovers. Instead of paying cash for an acquisition, a company can often provide at least one part of the cost by offering a share swap, as in the summer of 1985 when Guinness offered shareholders in Bell, the whisky distiller, paper worth considerably more than the market price of their own scrip. When an efficient company is taking over a dull one, shareholders of the latter are often only too glad of the chance of just such an easy escape route.

A final advantage of obtaining a listing is that the company attracts unsolicited funds. If they think you are doing well, any number of investors will buy your shares. Regular mention in the financial pages is useful publicity and, in the case of well-run companies, makes for easier relations with customers and helps when attempting to attract executive staff.

Going Public

When a company decides it would like to go public, it normally approaches a firm of stockbrokers through its accountants or bankers. There is then usually a lunch or dinner, a getting-to-know-you session at which little more will be achieved than a general understanding of the nature of the business, and its goals and aspirations. The directors of the company considering a listing will also obtain some idea of how, what is almost certainly a long operation, is planned.

Once contact has been established, and a decision in principle made, a partner in the firm of brokers will seek a total brief on the company – particularly its management structure, and strengths and weaknesses, its labour force, its present shareholders, its competitors, and, of course, a detailed study of full sets of accounts for the previous five years. Quite often this study will show that a listing quote is out of the question. In Britain investors and fund managers are spoilt for choice, and with the British Government offloading billions of pounds worth of assets in state enterprises, any company that does not offer first-class prospects will not attract support. To go down the road towards a listing, and to issue a prospectus, and then have to withdraw it, would be a costly mistake.

Assuming, however, that the feasibility study shows the prospect of success, the next stage for the stockbroker is to visit the company and its major plants or operations and to see it at work. This will usually be carried out by a senior member of the firm, under the supervision of a partner. The staff member will also try to visit competitors of the company, to seek another assessment, although the need for strict confidentiality makes this aspect of the study difficult. A firm of accountants, not the company's own auditors, will also be commissioned to carry out a thorough investigation.

All this will have to be done within three months, if a reasonable target for a listing is to be achieved. The next step is for the brokers to prepare a detailed proposal for the flotation, which will, in effect, form the blueprint for the day-by-day march towards the listing. The broker will suggest a price band within which shares might be offered – the decision on a firm price will come much later – and will set out a list of financial requirements which will have to be met and propose under-writers, who, at a substantial discount on price, will agree to purchase any shares if the float is undersubscribed. The company will usually be asked to pay off all major loans – for no investor is keen on picking up a load of debt – and to revalue all properties.

This stage completed, the next step is to decide how the

capital of the company is to be made available to the public. In most cases, this will be through the issue of a prospectus, offering the shares at a price expected to be lower than the price at which the company will start its life on the boards. In the main markets such a prospectus is published in full in *The Financial Times*, and, occasionally, other newspapers. The prospectus is, in fact, an offer for sale. It will detail the price at which shares will be available, and name any proposed restrictions on voting rights. The terms of sale will be set out, as well as the names and addresses of the auditors, stockbrokers, bankers, solicitors and directors. There will be a full description of its products or services.

Isotron, a company providing the only independent gamma radiation service in Britain, published just such a prospectus. It devoted thousands of words to an extremely detailed description of its technological processes, and its business prospects. A large part of the prospectus was devoted to the curricula vitae of the directors and senior employees, right down to site managers. There was a chapter on safety procedures, while over a page of closely-spaced print was devoted to publication of the independent report by accountants Peat, Marwick, Mitchell and Co. The reader was spared no detail, and the prospectus constituted an extremely thorough insight into the company.

Once the prospectus has been written, usually by the merchant bankers advising the company in association with the stockbrokers, the approval of the local exchange where the shares are to be listed must be sought. This is much more than a formality, and it is quite normal for questions to be raised on matters of detail for instance in London. The most pressing concern of the Exchange's Quotations Department is to see that the prospectus gives as full and accurate a picture as possible of the company and its prospects, and it is unlikely that a document will pass through unamended.

The terms of sale vary widely. Sometimes an underwriting firm of brokers will agree to buy all the share capital to be offered for sale on a given day, and then do their best to dispose of the shares to investors at a sufficiently higher price to offer them a profit. Sometimes the shares will be offered directly to the public by advertisement; where this happens the underwriters will only have to take on the shares left unsold, and if the issue is a success, may end up with no commitment and a useful underwriting fee.

Finding an underwriter is usually not a major problem, for all brokers have a list of those they can call upon, whether institutions, unit trusts, merchant banks or other financial groups. Underwriters do count, however, on the integrity and accuracy of a broker's recommendation. No firm of brokers can consider accepting the job of arranging a flotation unless it is convinced it is a sound investment.

An increasingly popular way of raising the cash is through public tender – used by bankers J. Henry Schroder Wagg and Co. in the Isotron case mentioned earlier. Here 3,290,088 ordinary 25p. shares were offered at a minimum tender price of 120p. a share, the system being that those prepared to offer a higher rate would receive the biggest allocation. Having received all the applications, Schroders were left with the task of setting a 'striking price', not exceeding the highest price at which sufficient applications were received to cover the total number of shares offered. A public tender was also used by Schroder's and Phillips and Drew in bringing Andrew Lloyd Webber's Really Useful Group to a full London listing in January 1986.

Obviously public tender is a system favoured by highly successful, confident and relatively well-known companies. It is not to be recommended if oversubscription is thought unlikely. It also avoids 'stagging' – a stag being the individual who buys new issues in the confident belief that oversubscription will lead to the price rising sharply on the day of listing.

Whether stagging occurs in the majority of cases when the tender system is not used depends, of course, very much upon the the price at which the shares are fixed for sale. Pricing can be the key to the whole issue. If prices are pitched too low, there will be a huge oversubscription, involving vast amounts of extra paperwork, the return of cheques, and the difficult job of selecting the lucky applicants to receive shares. The stags will have a field day. If, at the other extreme, the price is pitched too high, the issue will be a disaster, and months, even years, of work will be wasted. There have been examples of both, and where there is oversubscription, those applicants left out, or, as in the case of the Britoil issue, awarded derisory holdings, feel aggrieved, even bitter.

Fixing the price is not easy, however, because all companies are the prisoners of current events. A series of air crashes
could damage the price of the shares of a manufacturer of
jet engines, for instance. Inevitably setting the price is left to
the last possible moment, with brokers and bankers using
their experience to judge market conditions as D-Day
approaches. The forty days and forty nights before and after
the day of flotation are the busiest, when near frenzy envelops
the offices of those directly involved. It is not unusual for
the major people involved to camp in their offices during
much of this period, and certainly holidays are out of the
question. While the final offer documents are away at the
printers, they just pray that they have got it right.

Whether a company goes public through a full float or
sale by tender, it is a costly business. The experts needed –
lawyers, merchant bankers, accountants, brokers, and financial public relations men – do not come cheap, especially in
the City of London. There are few ways of doing it cheaper,
but one of them is to arrange what is called a placement. In
this case, the stockbroking firm buys all the shares and sells
them direct to its clients, avoiding the cost of dealing. This
method is used in small new issues in London or where there
is unlikely to be much public interest. But even here, the
Stock Exchange regulations stipulate that at least 35 per cent
of the company's issued capital must be in the placement,
thereby preventing directors from using the system as a ploy
to pick up some useful cash while still totally dominating the
company. At least one-quarter of the shares must also be
sold to the public on the stock markets, so that market
makers set a price, which helps when open dealings start. A
placement is much cheaper because the costs of advertising,
printing and professional services will be much less, and
there is no need for underwriters.

There is also the alternative of arranging an introduction,
but this way of obtaining a quotation in London is only
available to those companies that already have a wide distribution of shareholders, and where there is no immediate
intention of anyone selling out. No capital is offered prior
to listing, and it is therefore not necessary for the company
to go through the procedures described earlier, or to issue a
prospectus, although it is required to take an advertisement

to publicize the move. This method is most commonly used when a large foreign company decides to have its shares listed in London as well as on its home exchange.

Raising More Money

The Stock Exchange was founded to raise money for industry and to provide finance for great national projects such as railways and canals. It raised money with great success until World War II, and in the early post-war years it was the place where companies went for extra funds if they wanted to expand. Borrowing from the banks was, in Britain at least, considered expedient only for short-term finance. Borrowing from overseas – through instruments such as Eurobonds, and more recently ECU-denominated Eurobonds and Euronotes – was not even in the minds of those few City types who supported Jean Monnet's vision of an integrated European economic community. Raising money was the job of the Stock Exchange. Why go further than Throgmorton Street?

Things began to go badly wrong with the capital-raising function of the Stock Exchange when successive governments, mostly, but not exclusively, of Socialist persuasion, decided that the best way of paying for expensive public programmes was to tax the rich, which, to them, included almost everyone who did not belong to a trade union and pick up his wages in a brown envelope once a week. Income from share ownership was 'unearned income', and somehow thought of as less decent than interest obtained from a building society. Making a capital gain by selling one's own shares at a profit in order to pay for old age, school fees, or even a trip to the Bahamas, was regarded as sinful, and therefore had to be discouraged through extra taxation. Company taxes were raised, making it harder for businesses to fund expansion. And, in order to justify an ill-judged attempt to curb a free market for wages, 'dividend restraint' was imposed. With little point in investing either for capital growth or for income, investors followed the example of the trade union movement, and went on strike. In other words, they ceased buying shares, and held on to their holdings in such lame ducks as British Leyland, Dunlop, and Alfred Herbert, and watched them gradually run out of capital.

The political effect of the onslaught on the investor in the 1960s and 1970s was to bring to an almost complete halt a Stock Exchange system which allowed development capital to be raised, pluralistically, by a large number of individuals and institutions, and to replace it by a more costly system of finance through banks. It seems unlikely that the trend will ever be completely reversed, but in recent years there has been an encouraging revival of capital-raising on Stock Exchanges, to the benefit of both saver and entrepreneur.

Today business school studies by Nobel Prize winners Professor Franco Modigliani and Professor Merton Miller show that the costs of debt and equity financing are comparable. The cost of debt – of course – is easiest to measure: it is the interest paid by the company on its bank loan or bond. Assuming the company is a blue-chip it will pay a premium of about two per cent over a bond issued by a credit-worthy country like Britain or Germany.

The cost of equity is the dividend yield, which should be cheaper, but often is not. Dividends often depend on taxation policy. Raising money through the share markets through rights issues also strengthens balance sheets and prevents the kind of over-gearing that has forced many large companies into difficulty.

Sometimes companies will want to use both methods. For instance a British company may use a rights issue to fund a UK acquisition, but, if seeking to take over a European company, could use a foreign currency bond to match the currency of the target company's country.

What happens with a rights issue is that the holders of ordinary shares in a company are offered further shares at a discount, usually substantial enough to make it attractive. Under the rules, such new shares must be offered to existing stockholders in quantities proportionate to their holdings. This is known as a pre-emption right, which has been abandoned in the United States. A lively debate has been taking place in Britain over whether this rule is sensible. In many cases not all shareholders are willing, or even able, to take up the rights offer. So, under the present system, underwriters have to be found who will. As with new issues, pitching the price right is crucial. If a rights issue is undersubscribed there is a danger that the share price will fall, even if underwriters have been appointed, and this would defeat part of the objective of the exercise, which is to raise more capital. In the case of the 1985 Hanson Trust rights issue, when £500m was raised, the event was not without drama, and the Kuwait Investment Office obligingly took up the shares that some of the company's shareholders did not want.

The most important question for a company making a rights issue is to decide on the terms at which it will offer new shares. Normally this is done by offering the shareholders the right to buy a number of shares at a special price for each share they own. So, for example, in 1990 the British brewing group Bass sought to raise £558 million by giving its equity holders the right to buy one new share for every five they already owned. This is known as a one-for-five issue. In order to persuade shareholders to subscribe to a rights issue, the price has to be a worthwhile discount to the prevailing market price. But this does not mean that rights issues present shareholders with a bargain – an offer they cannot refuse. As soon as a rights issue has been completed, the price of the existing shares usually falls to reflect their dilution as a result of new stock on the register.

The small shareholder offered a rights issue is often in a Catch-22 situation. If he takes up the offer he has to dip into his savings and increase his risk exposure to the company concerned; in other words an additional investment is forced upon him. If he does not take up his rights he may sell them to a stockbroker for the difference between the rights price and the market price, but unless there is a substantial volume of shares involved the commission is likely to be prohibitive. If, as often is the case, you do nothing at all, the company will automatically sell your rights for you, and pay you the proceeds.

Rights offers are usually contained in a long and arcane document preceded with the suggestion that if you do not understand it you should see a stockbroker. Many people, particularly those who have not paid close attention to their investments or who have inherited equities, mistakenly throw these documents into the rubbish bin.

After the deregulation of Britain's financial markets at the time of Big Bang in 1986, many people believed that companies would move across to the American system of placements, described earlier. They reckoned without the big pension funds and life assurance companies, which dominate the British markets and who were jealous of their automatic right to get a slice of anything new going. These institutional investors formed a cosy cartel, which called itself the 'Pre-emption Group', and set itself the goal to protect at all costs the right of existing shareholders to get first refusal of any new shares. At the time this group was established, the British government was supporting a change in the rules, which would have allowed companies to raise additional capital directly from new shareholders. The Pre-emption Group frustrated this change by introducing a rulebook binding on all its members. One of the guide-lines was that in any issue of more than five per cent of a company's capital, the existing shareholders had to be given first call. Of course, as long as the institutions stuck to their own rules, their dominance in the market was such that nobody would be able to change matters. And, in Britain at least, so it has proved.

A rights issue is not cheap, which is one of the main arguments against this form of raising additional capital. First there are underwriting fees, paid by the company seeking to raise the money to the merchant bank or securities house managing the issue, and to those who have undertaken to buy any unwanted shares. These fees come to about two per cent of the amount of money raised. Then there is the paperwork – fees to lawyers, accountants and public relations consultants, plus the actual cost of printing and distributing the substantial amount of documentation necessary. Add to this the discount which must be offered to make the rights issue attractive – a figure of around 20 per cent is common practice – and it is easy to see why many a corporate financial director would rather go to see the company's bankers or, if it were possible, to arrange a placement.

An alternative to a rights issue is loan capital, which may be raised on the Stock Exchange either through unsecured loan stock or convertible stock. Loan stock is usually issued only by blue-chip companies; a company without a high rating would not find investors ready to buy it even at very high interest rates, and provide for the holder to convert all or some of the shares at a later stage to equities.

If a company is planning to modernize its plant to increase output and productivity, loan capital can be a particularly attractive vehicle. The interest paid is deductible before corporation tax is payable, so the company's tax bill is reduced. And as output rises, and hopefully profits, so does the company's share price, making it beneficial for the shareholders to make the conversion.

As with new issues, there are several ways in which a stockbroker can obtain loan capital for his clients. He can arrange for a full prospectus detailing the offer to be prepared, published and advertised, and wait for the response, usually stipulating preferential treatment to existing shareholders. He may, if he chooses, place the loan stock with institutions direct – unlike placements with new issues, where a proportion has to be offered on the Stock Exchange. Or he may limit the offer to existing shareholders, an unlikely course because especially attractive terms are usually necessary to get full support. A placement is usually much more efficient.

Then there is the bond market, of which the Eurobond market is the best known. Not long ago, only governments of stable and prosperous democracies and large international institutions such as the World Bank and the European Investment Bank would go to the bond market for funds, by issuing securities at good interest rates with maturity dates 10 to 20 years away. Mostly denominated in dollars, these securities offered large institutional investors an attractive hedge against the fall of sterling and against inflation.

The Unlisted Securities Market

Money can be raised for small and medium-sized go-ahead businesses through the junior Stock Exchange, better known as the USM, or Unlisted Securities Market. Similar markets have evolved in the United States and France, and the idea has widespread political support because such businesses are seen as major sources of job-creation, technological innovation and entrepreneurship. The high-interest rate environment of the past few years has compounded the financing problems of the growing company, but the USM does offer those who have a case and can present it well the chance not only of raising capital for their expansion, but also of becoming rich in the process.

In essence, joining the Unlisted Securities Market, which was only established in 1980, is a much simpler procedure than going for a full listing, but with many similarities. The cost is also much less – £50,000 for a medium-sized company with no major problems – and companies need only have had a three-year trading record.

The most common way of going to the USM is via a brokers' placing, whereby shares are sold directly by brokers to their customers, although 25 per cent have to be offered on the open market. A company seeking to join the USM discusses the prospect with his accountant, who mounts a thorough investigation into its affairs, and produces a prospectus. The most crucial factor in joining the USM is timing, since there are more capital seekers than funds available. If, during the one-year march towards a float, the company's financial advisers notice any downturn in prospects, they will almost certainly urge postponement.

9 Selling the Family Silver

'*It's like selling the family silver*' – Harold
Macmillan, speaking in the House of Commons.

'*I am not able to say myself whether it will be worth
all the labour involved in privatisation. I do not know.
I think we shall find out only a lot later on*' – Sir Denis
Rooke, chairman of British Gas.

'*Get it out . . . get it sold*' Kenneth Baker, when
chairman of the Conservative Party.

In its 1991 Budget the British Government came up with an
unusual announcement. The Chancellor of the Exchequer
said that it was planning to privatize a second tranche of
British Telecom, and that it was seeking 'bright new ideas'
from the High Street banks and building societies as to how
the shares on offer might be sold to the widest possible
public.

This relatively unpublicized statement betrayed the truth
of the earlier privatizations: that far too much money had
been spent with City middlemen only to find that much of the
equity had either ended up with institutions – the merchant
bankers, stockbrokers, lawyers, accountants and public
relations men having taken an enormous cut of the proceeds.

Privatization – pioneered by the Thatcher Government
on the idea of the management guru Peter Drucker – is a
philosophy which has swept the world. One by one governments have been divesting themselves of great state-owned
corporations. Britain has led the way in ridding the taxpayer
of the burden – and the public servant of the responsibility
– of hugh utility businesses like power and gas supply, telecommunications and airlines. Five years after people queued
in the streets of London to buy shares in British Telecom,
the Poles were forming their own lines to buy assets once
controlled by the communists.

Alas, in Britain a brilliant idea has been poorly executed with the result that very few members of the public have ended up with more than a handful of shares. Instead of encouraging saving, privatization bred stagging – making a capital gain by selling equity at a profit immediately upon acquisition. The issues were priced too cheap, and the City made a killing, leaving a nasty taste in the mouths of ordinary families who came to believe that share-trading was not for them.

It did not start off that way. I remember spending one wintry evening in the Conservative Club at West Houghton, an unpretentious Lancashire village in the drab industrial belt between Liverpool and Manchester. A group of women, two of them the wives of packers at a nearby baked-bean factory, were discussing the price of British Telecom shares. All had small holdings, following the Government's decision to sell off three billion shares in British Telecommunications plc to the public, in what had been the world's largest-ever share sale. The women agreed that they planned to hold on to their shares, even though they could sell out at a tidy profit. And they had become addicted to share ownership. Since the British Telecom issue, three of them had bought other shares. Said one: 'I have bought Marks and Spencer; I bought Rank Organisation and sold them again, and I am buying Dobson Park, because I think that will benefit from the end of the miner's strike.' 'I watch the prices every morning in the *Daily Mail*', said another, 'and sometimes I keep a watch on them through the day on teletext'. Neither the women nor their families had ever had shares before. 'I did not really know how to go about it; I did not know a reputable stockbroker, or how to go about finding one, and I certainly did not know the bank would do it. It was a matter of ignorance, really.'

The experience of West Houghton confirmed that a vein of popular capitalism existed to be tapped in Britain. Some stockbrokers argue that, even without privatization of great state monopolies at the initiative of the Government, new conditions had come about to make share ownership attractive to the individual. For the first time for over a quarter of a century, it was possible to generate a better return on capital invested in equities and other financial instruments than from that great middle-class – and heavily subsidized – bolthole, the family home. It was also true that some alleviation in death duties and other capital taxes had resulted in many couples in their late forties and early fifties inheriting a useful sum of money, which they chose to invest rather than spend on material possessions. When a City firm of stockbrokers conducted two investment seminars to canvass new business, one in London and the other in Preston, they obtained a significantly better response in the North.

Yet it is unlikely that the burst of interest in share ownership, particularly among the working classes, would have come about if the British Telecom float had not taken place, with its hype, touring road shows, television campaign and gimmicks like bonus shares and vouchers to help pay the phone bills.

Even more hype went into the sale in December 1986 of over four billion shares in British Gas, with the introduction to the nation's television screens nightly of an ubiquituous but enigmatic character called Sid. Clever if unsubtle advertisements by the Young and Rubicam agency urged viewers to 'tell Sid' about the opportunities for the public to buy shares in British Gas. One even had a pigeon fancier releasing his bird and saying 'there y'are my darlin', just go and tell Sid'. Right to the end of the campaign, Sid was never to be spotted; in the very latest advertisement a near-demented potential shareholder was seen climbing a mountain peak and peering through the mist crying 'Sid' at a shape that turned out to be nothing more than a startled sheep.

The British public gratefully accepted the offer like lambs – and why not? As with British Telecom, the Government had priced British Gas attractively and with a forthcoming election in mind – those who sold quickly were rewarded with a capital gain in excess of 20 per cent, and those who held the stock could look forward to cheaper fuel bills with the prospect of gas vouchers in addition to normal dividends. For every 100 shares bought, investors received a voucher worth £10 payable over a two year period.

Once British Gas was safely out of the way, the Government set about another major sale, that of British Airways. This was followed by British Steel, the nation's electricity industry, and the water authorities. The *Economist* saw it as 'the largest transfer of property since the dissolution of the monasteries under Henry VIII'.*

In France M. Chirac's Government planned to dispose of the state-owned banks, the Elf-Aquitaine oil group, and other nationalized concerns. One of the first enterprises to be sold was the glass manufacturer, St. Gobain, but then the socialists gained control and stopped the programme. The German Government returned Volkswagen to private ownership, while the Japanese sold Nippon Telegraph and Telephone, Japan Airlines, and the loss-making Japan National Railway.

Little, it seems, can escape privatization. In the United States some prisons are now in private ownership. They are more comfortable than Federal penitentiaries. And they are run at one third of the price.

* For a detailed account see Chapman, Colin, 1990: *Selling the Family Silver* (London, Business Books).

10. The Takeover Trail

'That's what a dawn raid is – you hit at dawn' –
Robert Holmes à Court.

Hardly a day goes by when the news headlines do not contain a major story about a takeover. Usually it is one large company bidding a billion dollar sum for another. Usually the bid is unwelcome: that is, the directors and management of the targeted company would rather be left alone. And what normally happens is that the investment bankers or stockbrokers to the predator company send a pre-printed letter, known as an offer document, to the shareholders of the target company, proposing to purchase their shares for cash or for stock in their own corporation, or a mixture of the two.

This inevitably raises the biggest question that arises with any takeover – value. How do you value a public company? One simple answer is market capitalization; the price of each share on the stock markets on a given day multiplied by the number of shares issued. Then all a bidder has to do is to pitch his offer sufficiently higher than the current price in order to persuade shareholders to set aside their long-term prospects with the existing board of directors in order to achieve a short-term gain.

But is the stock market price the right one? The prices of shares are fixed not by any measure of assets or even current profits, but by market-makers' perception of value based on all the information that might affect a company's future cash flow. All the company's financial statements are digested and assessed against competitive forces by scores of analysts – and their collective wisdom is pitted with the judgement of those who make markets and distilled into a share price. This sounds entirely plausible, but how can you then account for the fact that the world stock market as a whole on 19

October 1987 was worth only four-fifths of what it had been the previous day? Share prices can only really be the best guess at a value. An acquirer is not really buying the buildings, machinery and the workforce – he is getting what he thinks these are capable of producing.

As the Wall Street arbitrageur, Ivan Boesky, later to be gaoled for insider-trading, put it in 1985:

> An analyst may fully understand a company he is following, may even be able to forecast its future earnings with unmatched precision. Does that mean he can forecast its future stock price with any precision at all? Of course not. Price-earnings multiples averaged as high as 25 or so in the heyday of stock trading in the 1960s. In the mid-seventies these multiples had fallen to 6 and 7. Any stock market price is buffeted by sweeping market forces that are virtually impossible to predict with any reliability. These forces are often important: the growth rate of the economy, the course of interest rates, the international value of the dollar, the inflation rate, an overseas war, a presidential election. They also can be distressingly unimportant: this week's change in money supply, the Federal Reserve Board's sale of securities, its reversal of that sale the next day.

Nevertheless many large and significant public corporations have changed hands on the simple basis of share values. The predators have got what they wanted. The shareholders, presumably, were satisfied because they were able to take a profit and re-invest their money in other investments. But the companies and their staffs that found themselves with new owners were not necessarily better companies for the transformation. In some cases new blood made them more efficient, and more effective use was made of their assets. 'Making assets sweat' is one of the main justifications for takeovers. In many others the acquired company, its costs swollen by the expense of its own acquisition, has fallen apart.

I doubt whether there is any better example of this than what happened to Australia's three main television networks in the late 80s. The Nine Network was controlled by Kerry Packer, a single-minded entrepreneur with a reputation for seeking value in his investments and businesses. Run by a New Zealander, Sam Chisholm, later to become managing director of British Sky Broadcasting, it topped viewer ratings year after year. The Seven Network was owned by leading newspaper interests, including the Fairfax dynasty, proprietors of the influential Sydney Morning Herald and the Melbourne Age. And Network Ten was owned by Rupert Murdoch's family company.

Just before the Great Crash of 1987, Packer sold his network to the ambitious Alan Bond for $1.1 billion – a figure which represented a premium on its market worth, and was much more than its true value. Another eager entrepreneur with Hollywood ambitions, former financial journalist Christopher Skase, paid $780m – well over the odds – for Seven. And, as Australian law prohibits foreign interests controlling the electronic media, Murdoch was forced to sell Network Ten when he took American citizenship. He did so, at a handsome price, to some would-be media moguls who thought commercial television was, as Lord Thomson of Fleet had once put it, 'a licence to make money'.

All three newcomers crashed, their networks flattened not so much by an advertising recession as by the crippling interest rate burden of acquisition. In 1990 Packer bought back his Nine Network for one half of what he had been paid for it. The other two networks went into receivership, and at the time of writing are run by banks and firms of accountants. In each case the aspirants had made miscalculations about their future cash flows.

Not all of those carrying out takeovers continue to run the businesses they have bought. In many cases they sell the assets for cash. Asset-stripping is a popular occupation of those who believe that the stock markets often under-estimate the true value of companies, and they put their beliefs to the test by acquiring businesses and then breaking them up. This has frequently happened in the past when a company has a number of assets in its books – particularly real estate – which have not been written up with inflation. By disposing of the property, or by coming to a lease-back arrangement with a finance company, an asset-stripper can acquire tidy sums of cash. By the 1990s the activities of two generations of asset-strippers had sharpened up directors to the risk, though there is still a hard core of professionals on every continent who make money by spotting companies that are under-valued.

Despite the asset strippers and the ordinary everyday risks in mergers, such evidence as there is shows that takeovers often succeed in their objective of achieving real growth for the acquiring company. A study published in 1991 by McKinsey, the management consultancy, found that even cross-border acquisitions had achieved a high rate of success compared with other forms of corporate expansion.

McKinsey reviewed the overseas acquisition programmes of the top 50 companies in Europe, Japan and the United States – and found that 57 per cent were judged a success. However almost all the success stories related to a company merging with another in the same business. Most of those involving moving into non-core businesses failed.

Takeover Rules

In each country there are rules that govern takeovers. In some cases these rules are enshrined in legislation, in others they form part of a code, written or unwritten. In Britain the rules do not have statutory backing and have been rewritten three times since they first appeared as the City Takeover Code in March 1968. They are now enshrined in the litany of self-regulation that accompanies the 1986 Financial Services Act. Their observation is supervised by the City Takeover Panel, a group of twelve City elders whose modest secretariat is based on the twentieth floor of the Stock Exchange building. There is a director-general, two deputies, a secretary, and a few other executives. The permanent staff provide interpretations of the Code, but contested rulings and disciplinary cases are considered by the Panel itself, with the right of appeal to the Appeals Committee, which sits under the chairmanship of a retired Lord of Appeal. The Panel operates under the watchful eye of the Bank of England; it is usual for the majority of its staff to be on secondment from the Bank, providing a constant flow of fresh ideas.

The most important rule is that you may bid for up to 29.9 per cent of a company's shares before launching a full bid, but after that you must make a full offer for all the remaining shares, at the highest price you have paid for the purchases so far. This is to prevent a predator buying a company on the cheap, especially where there is a wide spread of share ownership.

Another fundamental principle is that shareholders must be treated evenly. 'All shareholders of the same class of an offeree company must be treated similarly.' Another rule provides that before an offer is announced, no one privy to the preliminary takeover or merger discussions is allowed to deal in the shares of either the bidding or target company. Once an offer is announced, the share transactions in all the companies involved must be reported by all parties to the City Takeover Panel, the Stock Exchange, and the Press. Companies defending a bid must not do anything without shareholder approval 'which could effectively result in any bona fide offer being frustrated, or in the shareholders of the offeree company being denied an opportunity to decide on its merits'.

The City Takeover Panel's executive staff are available throughout a takeover to advise whether the rules are in danger of being broken, as all bids for public companies, listed or unlisted, are strictly monitored. The staff work closely with the surveillance unit at the Stock Exchange to investigate dealings in advance of publication of bid proposals, the aim being to establish whether there has been any breach of the rules governing secrecy and abuse of privileged information.

If there appears to have been a breach of the code, the Panel staff invite the chairman of the company involved, or other individuals, to appear before the Panel. He or she is informed by letter of the nature of the alleged breach, and of the matters which the director-general will present to the hearing. These hearings are informal, there are no rules of evidence, and, although notes are taken, no permanent records are kept. The principal against whom the complaint has been made is expected to appear in person, although he may bring his lawyer with him. At the hearing he is expected to set out his reply, normally based on a document which should already have been produced in reply to the director-general's letter. If the Panel finds there has been a breach, the offender may be reprimanded there and then, or may be subjected to public censure with a press release distributed to the media, setting out the Panel's conclusions and its reasons for them. In a bad case, where the Panel feels that the offender should no longer be able to use the Stock Exchange temporarily or permanently, the case may be referred to a professional association, the Stock Exchange, the Department of Trade and Industry, or the City Fraud Squad.

The Panel is considered to be a legal entity, and the Court of Appeal has ruled that its decisions may, if need be, be reviewed by the Courts.

Making an Acquisition

Before considering how a takeover works, it is perhaps worth analysing some of the many and varied reasons for making an acquisition. The most obvious is that it is usually much easier and cheaper than starting a new business, except in the case of a product or service that is exclusive enough to depend, for its success, on the professional drive and energy of the entrepreneur and his team. If you have a product that will put your rivals out of business, you will usually be best served by building up the business yourself.

But if you wish to expand a business, a takeover is a useful route. Apart from anything else, it often enables you to use other people's money to achieve your ambition. A takeover can be a way of swallowing up the competition, and thereby increasing profit margins.

This was the case with many of the large takeovers in the early part of this century, when the first wave of mergers took place. Many of these were designed to set up large monopolies that could raise prices in basic industries such as steel, power and transport. Some of these were brought about by the legendary New York financier, J Pierpont Morgan. His biggest deal, in 1901, brought together 11 companies that accounted for half of America's steel industry to form US steel.

These days there are regulations to prevent monopolies through merger. In the United States there are strong anti-trust laws, and the European Commission is also vigilant against the development of new monopolies. New European rules coming into effect in September 1990 gave the Brussels Commission control over not just the major mergers and acquisitions, but also over small purchases made by mega companies. Mergers are subjected to Commission scrutiny where the combined world-wide turnover of the undertakings involved is more than 5 billion ECU, and where the Community-wide turnover of at least two of the undertakings is is above 250 million ECU.

Additionally Britain has a Monopolies and Mergers Commission.

In many cases, a takeover may appear to be the only way to fulfil ambitions of growth. Sometimes a takeover may be the result of egomania on the part of the chairman or controlling shareholder; there is never a shortage of new owners for Fleet Street newspapers, for instance, or for prestigious department stores, and breweries also seem popular. Sometimes the thrust of a takeover effort is to achieve a lifetime ambition, such as the attempt by Lord Forte and his son Rocco to gain control of the Savoy Hotel in London, an attempt that has always been thwarted by the antiquated and inefficient method of issuing preference shares.

Whatever the reason, there are usually only two forms of takeover: those that are uncontested, and those that involve a fight. But it is never as simple as that. There have been many occasions when a board of directors has decided to open merger discussions with a potential target rather than to proceed by stealth, only to find that the opposition is so great that all they have achieved is to give the other side advance warning to prepare for an assault. And there have been occasions when a contested battle has been so fierce and the cost of the operation so high that it might have been better to attempt to achieve the same result through negotiation.

Some takeovers are solicited. Many a company, for lack of progress or good management, feels that it would be better served if it were to be incorporated in a better run, and perhaps larger, business. I was once a non-executive director of a small public company in the retail motor trade. It had garages as far-flung as South Wales, Southampton, Birmingham and Lincolnshire, with different franchises in each. In one period of three months the Thatcher Government lifted interest rates three percentage points, thereby forcing the sale of stocked used cars at giveaway prices; an oil company decided not to renew the lease on the premises with the best showroom because they wanted a larger forecourt for petrol sales; and a strike at Vauxhall Motors dried up the supply of new cars for valuable orders at the main dealership. The directors, rightly I believe, sought to merge our company with a larger group better able to sit out what was to become a four-year crisis for the motor trade, and entered into discussions with a number of potential buyers. At one stage we were close to a deal. But then our shares slipped in the market; our creditors, seeing our market capitalization falling and rightly assuming that interest bills were rising, pressed harder, and the banks called in the receivers. The irony is that had it been a private company, without a listing, the company could well have weathered the storm, for the shareholders would have been obliged to stick with it through the bad times. Directors, of course, were not allowed to sell out, nor could they tell those friends who had supported the company, because that would have been classed as one of the most serious City offences, insider trading, punishable by heavy fines or imprisonment. So those that had risked their livelihoods lost their investment. It seemed rough justice at the time, but does illustrate an important point made earlier: the shareholders in a public company are much better protected than those in a private one.

There may also be hidden hazards in a solicited takeover. Take the case of Sinclair Research, a company built up by a technological wizard, Sir Clive Sinclair, credited with building the world's smallest portable television set, and the designer of an all-British range of microcomputers. Sinclair's drive and technological brilliance were not matched, however, by management skills, and many of his investments, such as his battery-operated vehicle, were less than successful.

In 1983, four years after it was founded, Sinclair Research had a market capitalization of £136m. In 1983 and 1984 the company was turning in profits of about £14m., and in 1985, although market conditions turned down due to a slump in the personal computer market, it was still looking to a useful profit. But in May of that year, serious cash flow problems became evident as stocks of £35m. of unsold goods built up, with suppliers demanding payment of their bills. For a while the main creditors, Thorn EMI and Timex of Dundee, agreed to hold off, and Sinclair's bankers, Barclays and Citicorp, increased the company's borrowing facilities. But, almost inevitably, the crunch came, and Sinclair turned to the bear-like clutches of Robert Maxwell, publisher of Mirror Group Newspapers, who, for reasons which have never been made very clear, made a £12m. rescue bid for Sinclair Research. Two months later, on 9 August 1985, it was all off. Maxwell announced that he was pulling out, saying the deal 'just did not gell', though he had no doubt that Sinclair computers were a 'fine product appreciated by millions'. Sir Clive Sinclair put a brave face on it, smiled wanly, and went off to see his creditors. It is a salutary lesson for those who see a takeover as salvation: you have to be sure you are really wanted.

With any takeover there are two stages: the preliminaries, which may take weeks and even months, and the active stage, when the bid is made and the offer digested and voted upon by the shareholders. Very few takeovers are the result of a whim, but are usually considered only after painstaking research, involving the company's solicitors, accountants and merchant banks, or other financial advisers.

Takeover specialists are at a premium in the City, and are paid enormous salaries. According to one leading firm of headhunters, Michael Page Associates, a senior director in the corporate finance department of one of the better known British merchant banks may expect to earn about £250,000 a year in salary and bonuses, while a junior director, who could be in his late twenties or early thirties, might receive £70,000 upwards. American companies pay more, but offer marginally less job security. For this, the specialists advise those either making or subject to a takeover on strategy and tactics, capital-raising where necessary, and public relations, often calling in outside specialists to assist. When the pressure is on, most advisers would expect to work 14 hours a day, as well as attending meetings at weekends. If their homes are outside central London, they would be lucky to see their families except at the weekend, and would almost certainly have to stay in hotels close to the City. One merchant bank maintains an apartment for its directors above an expensive West End restaurant. However, if you are seen dining with a new client, word soon gets out. Takeover advisers have to work under conditions of great secrecy, for an essential part of the takeover game is to anticipate your opponent's next move, and to outwit him.

However, for the merchant bank that can grab the lion's share of the business, the rewards are great, with takeovers and operations in the Euromarkets earning the greatest portion of its income. In 1985 fees from takeover activity earned City merchant banks a peak of £200m. Since then takeover activity has diminished. But there is still a scramble to be top dog, and a magazine, *Acquisitions Monthly*, now publishes a league table of the winners and losers.

Growth through Acquisition

Hanson Trust plc, which has grown into Britain's tenth largest company with turnover of £6.7 billion, started off selling fertilizers and renting out coal sacks. Much of its growth has been through acquisitions. In its 21-year history as a public company, Hanson Trust has lifted profits steadily from £140,000 to £252m. in 1985. The company maintains full-time senior executives in both Britain and the United States whose sole job is to earmark takeover targets, what one of the directors called 'culling', in other words raking through the performance records of industrial concerns looking for those that would benefit from the rigorous management style developed by the chairman, Lord Hanson, a tough York-shireman. Lord Hanson's methods are refreshingly simple. First the head office should be small; in his case a suite in London's Brompton Road, where there are less than 50 executives. Secondly there should be stringent financial controls: the centre operates like a merchant bank, draws in cash from the subsidiaries and insists on referral for expenditures over £1,000. Thirdly, and most important, the central management, including Hanson himself, leave the running of the businesses, which include Ever Ready, the batteries company, London Brick, the Allders stores group and airport duty-free shops, to those on the spot, limiting their own involvement to financial questions. Performance is guaranteed by generous incentive schemes, involving high cash rewards for those who achieve, not the best sales, the best image, or the lowest costs, but the greatest return on capital employed.

Both Lord Hanson and City observers reject any suggestion that Hanson Trust is an asset stripper. 'He does sell off parts of a company he takes over that he does not require', Robert Morton, an analyst with Barclays DeZoete Wedd told me, 'but that is because he knows what he wants, and there is no point in keeping the bits he does not want.'

During takeovers it is normal for managements of the 'losing' side to be replaced, and during the great insurance company mergers of the 1950s even clerical staffs feared redundancy, or a future with very little hope. This has now changed to some degree, and many acquisitions are made on the basis that the staff of the company acquired are guaranteed a job, and only top management are axed. This is the system operated by Hanson Trust. According to BZW's Morton:

> Board level moves on, and those lower in the company move up and benefit from the new incentives. Only very seldom does Lord Hanson go outside an acquired company for executives, normally finding there are people in the lower ranks who are pretty good.

In planning a takeover, it is essential to work out a strategy before going public. This usually means weeks closeted with financial advisers, and is a time when security is all-important. A stray document left in a photocopying machine, a loose word dropped to a friend in a bar, or even incautious lunching can lead to a leak. One paragraph in a newspaper can be enough to set the takeover target's shares racing ahead on the Stock Exchange, which could rule a bid out, or alert rivals to the possibility.

Furthermore, takeover strategy these days is not confined merely to obtaining enough shares in the targeted concern. In almost every situation, politics and public relations come to the fore. In some cases, they take precedence: for example, when United Newspapers, a medium-sized publisher of provincial newspapers with no national newspaper of its own, wanted to bid for Fleet Newspapers, publishers of the *Daily Express* and *Sunday Express*, it had first to seek the permission of the Monopolies Commission. It was even deemed impolitic to indicate a price, so Fleet shareholders had to play a guessing game for months.

The predator in a takeover enjoys one major advantage: it can always count on the full support of its management team, which usually has much to gain from taking charge of a larger organization. By contrast the management of a target company often finds itself in a difficult, even ambivalent, position; its loyalties are to its present board of directors, but its future, as likely as not, will lie elsewhere. It also has the burden of dealing with a worried staff, not to mention suppliers, distributors, and others with whom the company has close connections. And it has to continue to run the business. On the other hand, experience shows that shareholders will tend to stand by a business that has done well by them, unless those making the bid make an irrefutable case. Ralph Halpern of Burton had to fight long and hard and paid dearly for control of Debenhams, whose major shareholders, including its chairman, walked away with a tidy profit.

It is also true that the best defence against a takeover is to act before a bid, rather than afterwards – in other words, take action which will deter a predator from striking, such as selling off subsidiaries which do not fit the core of the business, or explain the company's strategy to analysts in such a way that the share price rises to reflect an accurate, rather than an undervalued, view of its stock. Once a bid is made, it is hard to do this, because any disposals or other capital restructuring have to be approved by shareholders.

When it is clear that a takeover bid is going to fail, what does the bidder do? There are occasions when a predator can come badly unstuck. Almost certainly he will have built up a parcel of shares in the company in which he is interested, although his bid will be conditional on sufficient acceptances to give him control. No one is expected to make an unconditional bid, but, once the fever is over, it can be difficult to recover the price paid for a block of shares on a rising market, and the bidder may be forced to take a loss. In such cases it is normal for him to arrange a placement through his brokers, in much the same way as when raising capital for his own concern. It is not unusual for the shares to be picked up by forces sympathetic to the company that has successfully defended itself against takeover, for the last thing directors want is an unstable market, especially if some of the allegations made in the heat of the moment seem likely to have stuck in the minds of the market.

A more interesting development occurs when an unsuccessful bidder actually walks away from the event with a large profit – not uncommon. Sometimes this can be achieved through barefaced cheek, especially if the subject of a bid has a group of directors and a large shareholder determined to hold on to their property at all costs.

This is what happened as a result of a visit on 20 November 1979 by the publisher Rupert Murdoch to his father's old office at the *Herald and Weekly Times* newspaper group in Melbourne, Australia, where he cheerfully greeted Sir Keith Macpherson, the chairman and chief executive, with the glad tidings that his News Group was about to present the Stock Exchange with the terms of a $A126m. bid for just over half of the company. Since the offer valued *Herald and Weekly Times*, the country's largest newspaper group, at $A100m. more than News Group, Macpherson suggested that the whole idea was ridiculous.

Perhaps it was; one newspaper later suggested it was like a snake trying to swallow a sheep, and similar metaphors were used when five years later, the entrepreneur, Robert Holmes à Court, made an unsuccessful bid for Australia's largest company, BHP, and was described, colourfully, as 'trying to rape an elephant'. Murdoch, however, knew what he was up to. He wanted the *Herald and Weekly Times* desperately – ever since his father, whose genius had built up the paper, had died, he had set his sights on it – but he suspected that he would not get it, even though News Group offered $4 a share, a premium of $1.26 on the market price.

His suspicions were correct. His bid caused panic at the headquarters of another newspaper group 400 miles away in Sydney. John Fairfax Ltd, a conservative family concern, had a minority stake in *Herald and Weekly Times*, and its newspapers were bitter rivals of Murdoch's. Apart from the extra power Murdoch would gain if he controlled HWT, he would become a partner of Fairfax in two other major enterprises, Australian Newsprint Mills, the country's only newsprint manufacturer, and Australian Associated Press, the national news agency, both controlled jointly by Fairfax and HWT. Fairfax instructed its brokers to buy all the HWT shares it could muster to thwart Murdoch, and the prices rose quickly to well above the $4 that Murdoch had offered. Within two days Fairfax had laid out over $A50m. and had acquired 15 per cent of HWT. The shares stood at $5.52. Murdoch knew that he was beaten, but he saw a lucrative way out. Instead of conceding defeat, he instructed his brokers, J. B. Were and Co., to continue buying shares but on a much more limited scale. At the same time he commissioned another broker, May and Mellor, to unload the 3,500,000 shares he had already purchased. The Fairfax people, convinced that Murdoch was still a buyer, snapped up the lot, paying top prices, only to face the humiliation of hearing that they had been outwitted and that Murdoch had quit, using one of his own newspapers to condemn the Fairfax 'rescue' of HWT as 'two incompetent managements throwing themselves into each other's arms at the expense of their shareholders'. Maybe, but the real point was that Fairfax was determined to stop Murdoch at any price, and paid dearly for it – for when the shares settled back down at a lower price, it had lost over $20m., plus the interest on the $50m. laid out to acquire the stock.

Ironically several years later Murdoch got his prize, as a result of some spectacular blunders by Warwick Fairfax, a junior member of the Fairfax family, whose dealings in the junk bond market lost him the empire his grandfather had built. Junk bonds are discussed later.

The trick is that your opponent has to hate the idea of losing his beloved company so much that he will pay almost anything to keep it. It is not a ploy that is encouraged by some of the more conservative bodies in the City of London, but it is fair game, and the best defence, if you are sure that the predator does not have the nerve or the money to go ahead with a bid, is to call his bluff, let him face the test of the market, and then take large advertisements in the financial press to deliver a wounding riposte.

In most contested takeovers the issue of who wins is decided by institutional investors, as the major shareholders. In Britain they are not quite as fickle as in the United States, on which more later, but increasingly the institutions are under pressure to perform. Stanley Kalms, whose Dixons electronics group won control of the electrical goods retailer Currys in 1984, accurately reflected the current attitude. 'Companies can only expect loyalty when their shares are performing well, and the market has confidence in the management.'

David Walker, chairman of the Securities and Investment Board, summed it up: 'I think that a business historian, looking back on the recent period, will stress the significance of the influence brought to bear on companies through the threat, if not the event, of takeover, and that many boards had an awkward and ambivalent relationship with their shareholders in many of these situations'.

The New Takeover Game

'Speculators may do no harm as bubbles on a steady stream of enterprise. But the position is serious when enterprise becomes the bubble on a whirlpool of speculation. When the capital development of a country becomes a by-product of the activities of a casino, the job is likely to be ill done', wrote John Maynard Keynes in 1936. 'What kind of society isn't structured on greed? The problem of social organization is how to set up an arrangement under which greed will do the least harm', said Milton Friedman, in 1973.

Those who promote takeovers – or believe that there should be no restriction other than a prohibition on monopoly – argue their case by saying that shareholders benefit by the maximization of share values. They also suggest that business is made more efficient, and necessary rationalization brought about, because large and indolent managements are forced to promote change, in order to survive. Be that as it may, the real reason for the frenzy of takeover activity in Britain and elsewhere is the desire of large numbers of corporate raiders to get rich.

As is usually the case, the Americans are well ahead when

it comes to exploiting the possibilities available to the corporate raider. Indeed, so sophisticated have US financial markets become that individuals are able to use an array of new financial instruments to play the same old games. One game, called appropriately 'Copycat', is to study the moves of renowned raiders like T. Boone Pickens, and to emulate them. You will be 24 hours behind, of course, but those who have followed this course in a bull market have seldom fared badly. Nor is there any need to use much of your own money; you can buy stock option for a fraction of the real cost, exercise the option when the price rises, and then sell out for a large capital gain.

It sounds like, and is, the stuff on which the 1929 Wall Street crash was founded, but now there are record numbers of Americans playing the share markets, and using sophisticated methods to do so. Scores of computer programs became available for individuals to analyse their portfolio performances, and to carry out 'what if?' analyses. Some programs are highly advanced, and can detect prices of related stocks that get out of step with each other. Armed with his personal computer and a copy of the *Financial Times*, the personal investor found he was almost as well informed as many professional investment advisers. There was no need to accept the low returns offered by his neighbourhood bank, or savings institution. Why should he not get the kind of interest, or strike the kind of deals, organized by the big boys? He wanted to climb on to the gravy train.

In 1980 only 49 million shares changed hands daily on the New York Stock Exchange. By 1991 this had more than tripled to 156 million shares. In this period prices rose sharply. Two-thirds of the rise is credited by analysts as being due to a feverish increase in takeover activity.

Much of this American activity was fuelled by borrowed money, in which the leveraged takeover has been a favourite technique. A corporate raider would take a modest position in a large company, wait a short while, and then offer to buy the entire stock by making a takeover bid. Where would the corporate raider's small company raise these billions of dollars from, you may well ask? Simple. He would approach a broker specializing in the art of raising junk bonds for worthwhile causes.

Where There's Junk There's Money

The man in the street might suppose that those proposing to take over a company have the wherewithal to do so. After all takeover merchants have always been painted as piranhas swallowing the small fry. This is not necessarily the case.

In the late 80s many takeovers were achieved with borrowed money, and in some instances this money was borrowed, indirectly, from the company that the predator was targeting.

Let me explain. Company X wishes to buy company Y, but has insufficient spare cash on its balance sheet to do so. Nor does it have enough security to offer its bankers, and it does not believe it can raise cash from its shareholders in a rights issue.

So instead it issues junk bonds, which are no different from any other interest-bearing security except that they carry a substantially higher than average interest rate. These bonds raise the capital required to finance a bid, and are normally secured against the shares of the company targeted. An investor in a junk bond normally does so on the basis that his money is only committed if the takeover bid succeeds. If it is successful the corporate raider issuing the bond can afford to pay the higher interest rates because he will have the assets of the newly-acquired company at his disposal. In other words the strength of the victim company's balance sheet is its own downfall. If the corporate raider fails and is unable to get enough shares in his target, it is a fair bet they will have risen in the market, and he will have made a sizeable capital gain.

The use of junk bonds was championed most heavily in the 80s by the Wall Street broking firm Drexel Burnham Lambert, where its greatest advocate was Michael Milken. By 1985 $27 billion worth of junk bonds had been issued, most of them through Drexels. In 1970 there had been only $7 billion worth of high-yield bonds outstanding, and most of that was for quality offerings. By 1989 the amount of junk that had been unloaded was $201 billion.

Many people imagine that the holders of junk were avaricious investors, dissatisfied with the more prosaic returns available on ordinary investments. They were not. At the beginning of 1989, 30 per cent of junk bonds outstanding in the United States were held by insurance companies, 30 per cent by mutual funds, and 15 per cent by pension funds. Many of them lost their money as the companies in which the junk was secured turned down. Drexels went bankrupt, and Michael Milken went to gaol.

An Australian Invades

The British public, even many British stockbrokers, viewed this activity in the United States with a kind of detached bemusement. City reaction was one of studied indifference; it could not happen here. But the City was awakened to leveraged takeovers in the autumn of 1985, when a relatively unknown Australian, John Elliott, came to London and bid £1.8bn. for Allied Lyons plc, a disco food and brewing conglomerate with a clutch of well-known brand names, including Skol lager, Double Diamond beer, Teachers whisky, Harveys Bristol Cream sherry, and Lyons Maid ice cream. Under the chairmanship first of Lord Showering, and then of Sir Derrick Holden-Brown, its record had been solid rather than impressive, and Elliott believed that he had the management skills and financial acumen to produce a better result for the shareholders.

Although his company, Elders-IXL, with interests in breweries, sheep farming, and financial services, was Australia's second largest industrial concern, it was only one quarter of the size of Allied Lyons. Indeed, Elders, with its powerful Carlton and United Breweries subsidiary, producers of the world-famous Fosters lager, was just the sort of company that Allied might have sought to gobble up itself had Australia's restrictive foreign investment laws made such a bid possible.

There were many in the City who welcomed Elliott's abrasive style, but there was deep concern as to the way the bid was mounted, for most of the funds were to come, not from Elders' own coffers, nor even from Australia, but from loans from a consortium of American banks. These banks, led by Citibank, were providing a facility of £1.23bn., two-thirds of the cost. The Government referred the bid to the Monopolies

Commission, not for any reason to do with monopoly, but because of concern at the financing arrangements. Whether the Commission, with its slow and arcane procedures, is the right place for a major issue of public importance to be debated is highly questionable; certainly the Government's decision was unfair to Elliott, and was seen by many as the achievement of some sustained lobbying. For a Government which purports to believe in decisions being taken in the market, it is strange indeed that it is unwilling to allow the decision to be made in the proper place – by the votes of Allied Lyons' institutional shareholders. Elliott abandoned the bid, and bought instead the Courage brewery group from another takeover predator, Lord Hanson.

Battle in the Courts

Across the Atlantic other forces were at work in the leveraged takeover game which were beginning to cause grave disquiet, particularly for those who subscribe to the old-fashioned view that since a public company is owned by its shareholders it is reasonable to assume that their interests come uppermost. The truth, of course, is a little different.

By an old quirk of fate, one of the victims in a case which was to become known as the 'poison pills' case was Lord Hanson. More than half of Hanson Trust's income comes from businesses in the United States, where Hanson's partner, Sir Gordon White, runs an identical operation. In August, 1985, Hanson and White identified a major American company as a suitable case for the Hanson treatment – the SCM Corporation, a solid if dreary conglomerate which manufactured outmoded typewriters, processed food, pigments and an assortment of other products. On 21 August, Hanson Trust offered $60 a share cash for SCM Corporation, valuing the company at $755m., well below its market capitalization. Robert Morton, an analyst with brokers De Zoete and Bevan, told me at the time that this was 'in the mould of Hanson acquisitions: SCM is exactly the kind of company he goes for, a company which has already undergone a great deal of rationalization and sorting out,

which perhaps has not been fully realized by the shareholders'.

The SCM management was horrified. Here was this lord
from England buying their company at rock-bottom value.
By all the precedents, it was clear that, before they knew
where they were, they would be looking for new jobs. Fortunately for them the board saw matters the same way, rejected
the Hanson bid, and refused even to talk to Sir Gordon
White, despite several invitations to do so. It hastily called
in its financial advisers, the redoubtable New York firm of
Goldman Sachs.

Curiously, however, it was not Goldman Sachs that came
to the rescue of SCM's beleaguered management, but Wall
Street's largest broking house, the New York financial conglomerate Merrill Lynch Pierce Venner Smith and Co. Merrill
Lynch's capital markets division, headed by a young go-
getter, Ken Miller, was hungry for new business, and skilful
in organizing what has become known as leveraged management buyouts. Within a few days, Miller and his team had
come up with a means whereby, at the stroke of a pen,
Hanson could be thwarted, the SCM management could save
their jobs, and Merrill Lynch would receive a large fee.

So it was that on 30 August, only nine days after Hanson's
bid, a new company was announced – legally a partnership
between the SCM Corporation's management and Merrill
Lynch, but funded by the Prudential Assurance Company of
America. It offered $70 a share – $10 more than Hanson –
for 85 per cent of the SCM shares, and promised to buy the
rest out of SCM profits at some future date, through the
issue of junk bonds, which, it was hoped, would trade at
about $70. A confidential Merrill Lynch paper described
the deal as representing 'one of the most asset-rich LBO
opportunities we have ever encountered'.

The wily Merrill Lynch team hoped that Lord Hanson
would withdraw, but they took sensible steps to protect
themselves, and their fees, if he did not. If Miller pulled this
on off it would be the first time that a leveraged management
buyout had been successful against a tender offer for cash.
But there was a risk, so a clause was written into the contract
providing for a $9m. fee should the bid be topped and the

arrangement terminated, in addition to the basic fee of
£1.5m. for fixing the deal in the first place.

Lord Hanson proved their fears justified. On 3 September,
Hanson Trust increased its offer to $72 a share. Unlike the
first offer, which valued SCM at a bargain basement price,
this was a much more attractive offer for shareholders. For
a start it was all in cash, with no waiting around for junk
bonds and future profits which might or might not appear.
For the SCM management, however, if presented the same
problem, the prospect of the sack, made even more certain
as a result of their tactics in signing up with Merrill Lynch,
and handing over $9m. of the company's money in fees. Sir
Gordon White did, however, hold out an olive branch. On
10 September, after several failed attempts by telephone to
contact SCM's chairman or board, he sent them one further
invitation: 'We believe it is in our mutual interests, including
those of your stockholders, management and employees, that
we should meet promptly'.

There was no reply, for, behind the scenes, Miller and his
team had again been hard at work, advancing another, much
more ruthless, way of frustrating Hanson's ambitions. Mean-
while the $9m. fee had already been placed in escrow. The
new plan was to strip out of SCM Corporation its two most
potentially profitable business, in the sure knowledge that
the Englishman would either lose interest or be left with a
crippled business.

This tactic has become known as the use of the 'poisoned
pill', although a more appropriate metaphor might be that
of a scorched earth policy. In this instance, the SCM management and Merrill Lynch increased their leveraged buyout
offer to $74 a share, but subjected it to a new condition; if
Hanson or another other party got more than a third of
SCM shares, Merrill would have the right to purchase the
two most thriving parts of the SCM Corporation – the pigments and processed food business – at knockdown prices.
The business would then be run by the same SCM management. These two businesses were to become known as the
Crown Jewels, for Merrill Lynch obtained the options for a
total of $430m. against the SCM board's own valuation of
$400m. for the pigments business and $90m. for the foods
division. For organizing this neat new arrangement, Merrill

Lynch took a retention fee of $6m., investment banking fees of $8m., and dealer-manager fees of $2.75m., in addition, of course, to the $11.5m. already paid.

The next morning Hanson Trust withdrew its $72 a share offer, and spent $200m. buying SCM shares on the New York market; within a few hours it had acquired 25 per cent of the company. But on 16 September Merrill Lynch acted again. With the Manufacturers Hanover Bank acting as agent, it put the shares of the crown jewel subsidiaries in escrow, and apparently beyond Hanson's reach. At this point the lawyers took over, with the action moving to the New York District Court in lower Manhattan. In the end Hanson Trust lost the case, but the verdict was reversed in the subsequent appeal.

Discussion in the United States has ranged over whether the law courts are really the place to decide such matters, as well as whether the frenzy of takeover activity wastes scarce investment capital, inhibits innovation, and forces managers to sacrifice long-term goals to the next quarterly profits sheet. Kathryn Rudie Harrigan, Professor of Strategic Management at the Columbia University Business School, talked to me about the increasingly common tendency for stock market takeovers to be decided in courts of law:

> It is just one more in a string of devices that managers and their investments bankers have come up with to avoid being taken over when they do not want to be.

Is this new trend likely to be damaging to shareholders? Professor Harrigan thinks perhaps not, in that values are often forced up by what is essentially a game:

> It is a game, and it is a game that is played with great ritual, and is being played in many, many companies these days. It is often cheaper to acquire something than it is to build it from the ground up.

But she does believe that business will suffer in the end:

> I think it is damaging to the long-term health of the business, because when you are so busy satisfying these short-term requests of the financial community, who are looking for instant

gratification from their investment, you often cripple the long-term ability of the company to be able to reposition itself to remain competitive in a changing environment.

Professor Harrigan also believes that the concepts of poison pills and crown jewels could be exported to Britain, now that the Big Bang has revolutionized the way the Stock Exchange works:

> The two capital markets are becoming very similar in the way that people operate within them, and the kinds of expectations they have of the companies whose equities they hold. And more and more of the equities are held by institutional investors, who have this kind of short-term expectation, and they want to see this quick pay-off on their investment. I think the kind of behaviour we see here, with these leveraged buyouts, will undoubtedly be appearing also in your stockmarkets.

As takeover battles become more complex, it becomes increasingly likely that more and more lawyers will be drawn into the corporate financial area. There are, however, likely to be strict limits placed on the way acquisitions can be financed by debt. While the British Monopolies Commission deliberated privately on the issue – in the context of the Elders-IXL bid for Allied Lyons – the Federal Reserve Board in Washington decided to extend its long-standing margin requirements to take in corporations that are set up only as entities to sell debt and finance the purchase of shares.

The Wall Street crash of 1929, brilliantly chronicled by John Kenneth Galbraith in his book of the same name, was brought about by excessive share speculation paid for with borrowed money. If prices were going up by leaps and bounds, why not borrow? The trouble was that when everybody did it, it spelt ruin. To avoid repetition the Federal Reserve's regulations have long dictated that loans for share purchases cannot exceed 50 per cent of the value of the stock being bought. But the rules have not applied to bonds, and until 1986 there was nothing to prevent a shell company being forced to raise debt finance through junk bonds, to fund a leveraged takeover.

One example that alarmed the US authorities was the successful move by Pantry Pride, a relatively unknown supermarket chain in Florida, to take over Revlon for $1.8bn. Pantry Pride, with the help of Drexel Burnham, issued $700m. of junk bonds. It knew that the funds generated by its own operations would not be sufficient to meet its new debt service and dividend operations, but once it had acquired Revlon it was able to finance these obligations from the sale of a number of Revlon assets.

'Abuses by some banks and financiers are feeding a take-over frenzy that strikes at the economic well being of this country', one potential victim of a leveraged takeover wrote to Paul Volcker, then the chairman of the Federal Reserve. 'They are engaging in stock and bond and credit schemes reminiscent of those of the 1920s – but on a multi-billion dollar scale.' By extending the 50 per cent rule to shell companies, Volcker did not rule out using such tactics. He has just made them less attractive – 50 per cent less attractive, in fact. For those that have the stamina to engage in it, it is still an attractive pastime, so long as you can stay ahead of the game.

11 Fast Money

Within microseconds of the price of a major company changing on any of the major markets, investors anywhere in the
wired-up world will hear of it. Financial news travels faster
than anything else.

For the full-time dealer in a broking firm or institution
there are on-line services which provide prices in real-time.
These, of course, are very expensive, but for market-makers
competing with each other they are an essential tool of trade.
The professional investor normally makes do with less expensive electronic services, which nonetheless provide essential
figures and information within five minutes of its release.
Dow Jones, founded by Charles Dow, a self-effacing reporter
on Wall Street who became the first editor of the *Wall Street
Journal*, is one of the world's leading information providers,
rivalled by Reuters, the British news agency started in 1851
by Paul Julius Reuter using a flock of carrier pigeons.

The Reuter Monitor contains about 2,500 pages of information, which are regularly updated by some 400 contrib-
uters. Instruments covered include straight and convertible
bonds, stock market indices, government and domestic
bonds, warrants, swaps, Euronotes and commercial paper.
Reuters also maintains an accessible data base, which covers
almost 5,000 Eurobond issues, in all major currencies.

Another service, Money 2000, provides a complete and
continuous overview of market movements and relevant factors affecting currency futures and options, interest rate
instruments, and stock index futures and options. Equities
2000, launched in May 1987, provides a real-time quotes
service covering equities, options and futures fed from stock
exchanges around the world.

Some of the Reuters news services have become interactive
– all or some of those who subscribe may use the terminals
that are provided to trade on the information made available.
Reuters currency services, for instance, link via satellite and

high-speed cable foreign exchange dealers in more than 110 countries – and have become the world's foreign exchange market. Money dealers may access real-time information on currency and deposit rates, employ a range of graphs and other analytical aids to help their decision-making, and then use the Reuters network to complete their transactions with counterparties. Regardless of location, a dealer can contact another elsewhere in the world in no more than four seconds. The average connection time is two to three seconds. To contact a counterparty in Tokyo, a dealer in London or New York simply presses a four-letter code, or a single-key macro code stored in an address abbreviation facility. This facility also stores frequently used phrases or sentences, and can instruct the system to find the first free counterparty on a list and send a prepared message. An automatic print-out records details of every transaction for both dealing parties. The network is secure and private.

Roughly a third of the world's foreign exchange is done through Reuters' dealing screens, and another third is transacted by telephone after consulting a Reuters monitor. Clients, who include most of the world's bank, pay a rent for the screen and a fee.

After introducing a Eurobond service in 1975, Reuters continues to develop a number of other interactive services to meet the needs of international capital markets, and constitutes a major challenge to stockmarkets that do not move swiftly to offer electronic on-screen dealing. Already its wholly-owned Instinet trading service in the United States is used by professional investors to trade 8,000 American equities. Instinet is legitimized because its subsidiaries hold membership of seven major United States securities exchanges, as well as the International Stock Exchange in London. The network has more than 750 terminals connected, and in 1977 transacted 1.44 billion shares, with each transaction executed in seconds. Most of these services are of interest or use only to the major professional investor or institution.

Then there are a host of telephone services. These range from the relativity unsophisticated, which enable you to make a phone call and hear a recording of the latest major share prices, to several well developed schemes where once you are connected to the database, you key in a code from your telephone handset and hear the latest price of the share or unit trust identified by the code. Subscribers are given a free directory listing the codes.

Television has taken over from the printed word as the first conduit of financial information. In the United States there were two networks dedicated to business and financial coverage, one of them maintaining a permanent camera on the New York Stock Exchange's ticker, so viewers who leave their sets on can be in constant touch. CNN, the Cable News Network available in over 100 countries, has hourly financial updates, and a number of in-depth financial programmes, including *Moneyline*, the most watched business show in the United States, and *World Business Today*, a co-production with Financial Times Television, produced in London. In Europe Sky News updates its *International Business Report* several times a day and the BBC has a morning business show, while in Japan there are several networks dedicated to the requirements of those following the markets.

So there has been an explosive growth in the financial information industry, which has increased the pool of knowledge about the financial markets and the companies traded there to the point where it is now well beyond the capability of one person to digest it all. Gone are the days when a stockbroker would sit in his first class rail carriage from Sevenoaks to Charing Cross and comb through the pages of *The Financial Times*, working out his share tip of the day. Once at the office, he would telephone his friends and relations, and they would all be on to a good thing. A former City Editor of the *Daily Express* once told me that he had bought a house in the stockbroker belt and always travelled in a first-class compartment so as to be able to pick up such juicy tit-bits from those who were habitually on the same train. The journey home would usually be spent in the buffet-car where, over a beer or two or three, the successes of the day and the tips for tomorrow would be discussed.

In the late 1950s, the City Editor was a man of great authority, with an arrogance that could come only from having a considerable following of small investors. I remember Patrick Sergeant of the *Daily Mail* informing readers, just before leaving for his annual holiday one August, that they should not buy or sell any shares until after he got back. Patrick was not amused when he returned to find an anonymous telegram saying: 'Now that you are back, can we buy? – signed Pru and Pearl.'

City Editors also conducted their business with a certain panache. They would arrive in the office after a long lunch, smelling of port and accompanied by a cloud of cigar smoke. Even today, several Fleet Street City Editors are provided with dining rooms, at which they entertain City luminaries and government economic ministers. One or two others have a regular table provided for them at the Savoy Grill.

But nowadays most media organizations save for the popular tabloids have an army of financial journalists reporting on the markets.

Then there are specialist publications, which include the *Financial Times*, *Wall Street Journal*, *The Economist*, *Investors Chronicle*, *Money Observer* and *Financial Adviser*.

In the printed word the *Wall Street Journal* is the best guide for the share investor in the United States, while the *Financial Times* leads in Europe. Those serious about the markets should take both.

Those beginners who wish to take an interest in the markets should consider buying *How to Read the Financial Pages*, by Michael Brett (Business Books), which explains what the various indices and figures are and how they should be interpreted.

But if the press has made great strides in the last decade in the spread and depth of its financial coverage, it is no longer the only, or even the major, source of information. The real explosive growth in the financial information industry has come from stockbrokers themselves, with almost all the major broking houses running their own publishing operations. These brokers pride themselves on being able to get their publications out fast. On Budget day, for instance, some broking firms, as well as a few firms of accountants, will have their analysis of the Chancellor's measures in the hands of important clients before the newspapers.

Brokers' publications fall into two categories. There are regular weeklies or monthlies which contain a detailed review of the major economies and their financial markets, and offer a number of recommendations. Their forecasts have a high reputation for accuracy, usually better than the Treasury's.

Amongst the regulars are Morgan Stanley's and Phillips and Drew's monthly outlooks, which are always good reading. There are regular specialist publications also, such as Salomon Brothers' *Financial Futures*, and *Options Analysis*, Yamachi's *Investment Report*. Then there are sector or subject reports, which look at either a company or an industry in great detail, and come up with recommendations.

In contrast with these worthwhile publications are the tip-sheets. All you need to be a tip-sheet publisher is a word processor, a jobbing printer, some stamps, and a bit of flair. You also need to be licensed. Some of these tip-sheets tend to be a little self-indulgent, but there must be a market for them, otherwise they would not exist.

Investor Relations Managers

The rise of the specialist broking press has been such that the financial directors of large companies, and their public relations men, often spend more time wooing brokers' analysts than talking to financial journalists. A new corporate breed has emerged, the investor relations manager, whose job it is to keep both institutional investors and analysts informed of the favourable aspects of the company. They now have their own body, the Investor Relations Society. Many of its members have lavish expense accounts, and jet in and out of two or more European capitals a day, expending great energy and charm on their subjects. Things can, however, go wrong. I remember the investor relations executive at Olivetti wringing his hands at an unfavourable broker's circular on his company written by a very presentable woman analyst, and crooning down the phone: 'How can you do this kind of thing to me?'

In recent years increasing attention has been paid by the major European companies to soliciting investment in the United States, and those who have neglected this aspect of financial public relations have done so at their cost. Had Unilever, for instance, been prepared to take a stronger public profile in the United States, the outcome of its important takeover bid for Richardsons-Vick might have been different, and the company might not have fallen to arch-rival

Proctor and Gamble. Before, during, and after the bid, the Unilever board declined to talk to either *Forbes* or *Fortune* magazine, nor did they take the opportunity of appearing before the New York Society of Security Analysts daily lunch, which is now televised and distributed by satellite to over 360 leading portfolio managers and almost 1,000 of the nation's top analysts by the Private Satellite Network.

A contrast is provided by ICI, which maintains a full-time investor relations executive in New York to keep analysts at both institutions and broking firms up to date with the company's financial affairs. Some of the information is printed material, but another aspect of the job is to organize an annual road show to five American cities. There are also quarterly meetings allowing all major US analysts to meet the company's finance director and other top members of staff, and visits are arranged for those who wish to tour ICI's operations in Britain.

Investor relations specialists are now having to deal with an extra medium – specialist television. In the summer of 1985 PSN, a company headed by William Miller, a former Treasury Secretary and chairman of the Federal Reserve Board, and backed by major Wall Street finance houses, launched the Institutional Research Network (IRN), a private television network for the professional investment community. Each day, publicly traded corporations, investment bankers and research brokers provide financial programming to the analysts, portfolio managers and investment officers of the institutional investment firms that shape world financial markets.

The network has already been used by major corporations for a variety of planned and last-minute presentations, such as takeover battles, discussion of quarterly earnings, new product announcements, new management introductions, and chief executive interviews. Merrill Lynch has used the network to link Sheraton ballrooms across America so that invited interested investors could question their top portfolio investment experts in New York.

In Japan a similar network is run by the Spacewave consortium led by Mitsubishi. This brings live hearings from Capitol Hill to the subscriber's desk. It also shows specialist programmes on sectors of the European market made by Financial Times Television in London.

In the future the merger of telecommunications technology with that of the personal computer is likely to lead to those with PCs being able to access a business television network in one of the windows on the screen. Thus an executive working in one window on a spreadsheet or a business report will be able to keep one eye on another window carrying an international news service like CNN, able to size it up to full screen the second anything important happens.

It remains to be seen when such a network will be operational in London. When I canvassed such a possibility in the City, the caution of the financial establishment emerged. 'I cannot imagine brokers wanting to watch television in the office', said a partner in a major firm, forgetting of course, that many of his staff do little but stare at screens containing information. 'I do not think the City would want to go in for this kind of show business', said another, again totally missing the point. He had just come from lunch at the Butchers' Hall at which Pirelli's president had made a long presentation, using slides and other visuals which were indecipherable, and at which questions had to be cut short for lack of time. Most of the analysts present complained, not about the cooking, which was excellent, but about the quality of information available. Had they been able to see the Pirelli chairman, American style, in a well assembled but no-frills television production, they would have learned more.

The Analysts

The profession of stockmarket analyst is one of the greatest growth areas in the City. Once the analyst was the office introvert, who spent his day hidden from view in a corner behind a pile of dusty papers, fretting over obscure charts while his broking colleagues got on with the business of trading shares.

Securities analysts have now formed an industry in their own right, and have their own professional body. It is a highly competitive business, and one in which the rewards can be considerable. There are even annual contests for best analysts, and broking firms, sector by sector. The best known survey, now the Extel Ranking of UK Investment Analysts, was started in 1973 by Continental Illinois, and is based on a detailed questionnaire sent to investment managers of the major institutions. Only four out of ten bother to reply in detail, but this still makes almost 100, with over £400bn. of funds in their care, and the survey is self-perpetuating, as the winners can count on many a new job offer and a stream of telephone calls from journalists, merchant bankers, accountants and others also anxious to tap their expertise.

The top ten broking firms in London together employ over 650 analysts, of which 220 cover European and overseas sectors. Of the total 86 are women. Amongst all firms one in eight of a total of 1,300 analysts are women.

The Extel survey also revealed how specialist analysts have become. The typical analyst covers three or four sectors of the market, and studies 38 companies. Their average age is 32.5, and the typical member of the fraternity will have spent six and a quarter years in the business, and three and a half years with his or her firm. Fundamental research and field trips take up to two thirds of their time – and they spend a surprising 22 per cent on marketing activities, particularly talking to the media. This partly explains why analysts, particularly those who appear frequently on radio and television, are not universally admired, particularly by the chairmen of companies upon whose operations they comment.

The job of an analyst is part office-based, part on the road. He or she – and there are an increasing number of women in the business – has access to high technology, particularly numerous computer programs designed to make the postulation of future trends easier. An analyst will also spend a lot of time on the telephone asking questions, as well as attending briefings and seminars. In recent years it has become customary for companies, particularly large companies, to make life as comfortable as possible for analysts, transporting them en bloc or individually to expensive country hotels, where it is possible for them to socialize with directors and senior management as well as to talk shop. A thorough briefing of analysts just before a company's results are published can be crucial in getting a good press, for increasingly newspapers are dependent on the views of ana-

lysts for comment. Expectations can be lowered, if profits
are going to be bad, and vice versa. Some companies choose
an exceptionally attractive venue for six-monthly or yearly
meetings with analysts; Olivetti's Carlo de Benedetti, for
instance, favours Florence, where the men and women from
broking houses across Europe can sample art and Tuscan
wine. Pre-privatization, British Airways flew opinion-makers
in the City to a variety of overseas locations in the old but
not mistaken belief that the further away from home the
closer the mind might be concentrated on the subject in hand.

Often it is the City public relations firm which oils the
wheels of the information industry function. Financial public
relations companies like to think that they are a cut above
their contemporaries in the West End who deal with products
and services, and they probably are. Their senior people
certainly behave better, and have larger expense accounts.
Their role is also much more important. There are legal
obligations on companies who make financial changes to
inform the press, and someone has to ensure that announcements are hand-delivered round the City at the right time,
usually in late afternoon. There can be no question of sending
out details of an acquisition, or a rights issue, on an embar-
goed basis.

But City PR advisers are no mere messenger boys. In many
cases they are the eyes and ears of a company chairman
and, occasionally, his voice. Some company chairmen are
gregarious and well-connected individuals, able both to project a positive image and to be sensitive to public opinions.
The majority are not. A good PR person will be able to
keep the chairman and directors informed of shareholders'
opinion, what the newspapers are saying and, increasingly
important, an assessment of political and Whitehall and
Brussels opinion. If needed, he will be able to lobby politicians on the company's behalf. In major takeover activity,
or in rights issues, the public relations man will also become
a valuable aide to merchant bankers and stockbrokers.

Financial Advisers

With such a wealth of information available, to whom do today's investors turn for advice, and from whom can they obtain the most reliable advice? It is an obvious question, and it is perhaps the one that is most frequently asked by those with more than a few pounds to invest. It is also one of the hardest questions to answer.

One quite correct answer is no-one. In the end the investor, whether the chief investment manager of a large insurance company or a widow in Worthing, has to make the decision as to which is the best vehicle for improving the value of his or her savings. It is possible, even for those who do not consider themselves financially literate, to have cheap access to a great deal of information, and even that is sometimes of less use than a hunch or an everyday observation. For instance, anyone who has watched the development of Britain's High Streets over the past ten years will have noted the rise of Marks and Spencer. Shopping at Marks is not cheap, but its goods are of high quality, and its stores are full. Goods are seldom discounted, not even when adjoining stores are holding cut-price sales. Anyone reading the details of the M and S credit card, and its very high interest rate, and reading in the press of the large number of cardholders, will see that profits from this source will grow. You may not make a quick profit on M and S shares, but they will grow, along with British Telecom, British Airways, and smaller concerns like Forte.

But this is to dodge the real question. To whom can one turn? A bank manager, stockbroker, accountant, building society manager, perhaps. All have their place and purpose, but none of them is necessarily a good investment adviser. Today's bank managers prefer to lend money than to give investment advice, steering customers in the direction of inhouse unit trusts, which, with few exceptions, have not been the best performers. Accountants are useful tax advisers, and usually save you the cost of their fee, but when one seeks investment advice from them, they can start talking about complicated accountant-run pension schemes for the self-employed, and property trusts. Building society managers live or die by the balances on deposit in their branches, so it is not easy to accept their views as impartial. This leaves stockbrokers, who can be either good or bad advisers, but mostly are a mixture of both.

Regrettably very few large stockbrokers seem to want to service individual investors, and an increasing number of firms will not deal with them at all, unless the clients are very rich. This short-sighted approach is in contrast to the interest shown in small investors in the US, where share shops are common. But it is typical of the attitude of many in the City towards the average member of the public, and it is one reason why interest in individual share ownership is not high. Contempt for the small investor is one of the saddest consequences of recent years and it has been fostered particularly by the large conglomerates now owned by international banks. Most of the large brokers found that servicing small investors was tiresome and unpopular. If you had only a modest sum to invest, you were lucky to find someone prepared to buy for you, and you knew that they would never advise you to sell, unless you gave them discretion over your account, in which case they would trade with little rhyme or reason, a process, taken to extremes, known as 'churning'. Half the time small investors would not know who to ring at a broker's office, and if they discovered a friendly soul, he would be gone within weeks.

Some large broking firms began to operate a two-tier broking service – one for rich clients and the institutional investors and another 'no frills' service for the rest. Barclays de Zoete Wedd disenfranchised some of the old account holders of De Zoete and Bevan and enrolled them in Barclayshare, provided, of course, they opened an account with Barclay's Bank. Natwest started Brokerline, with a minimum commission of £25 per transaction. These services operate only by telephone – and personal investment advice is not included. They are for those who know what they want to buy and sell, who wish to do so in business hours only, and who have the fortitude to wait to make a connection. Getting through to any of them is not easy. Fortunately, there is an alternative for the small investor – the provincial sharebroker. Many believed that small regional brokerages would disappear after Big Bang – as the heavy battalions mopped up the business. The reverse has been the case.

Albert E. Sharp, the Birmingham-based firm, started a highly efficient telephone brokerage, Sharelink, for small investors, and introduced a Sunday service. It managed to pick up quite a lot of institutional business as well, particularly from medium-sized companies who were unimpressed by the arrogant approach of many of the City firms. It also introduced a new commission rate – starting at 2 per cent for the first £2,000, but then falling to only 1.25 per cent on the next £6,000 and only 0.25 per cent on larger amounts.

It may well be that Britain will follow the example of the United States. There, sharebrokers take their business to the public, and in almost every prosperous suburb there will be one or more open-plan broking offices, laid out rather like a large travel or estate agent, where members of the public may call, enjoy a cup of coffee, and discuss their investments with a consultant. There is plenty of literature available, including both brochures and financial magazines; Wall Street prices run continuously on television monitors, and there is a friendly and unpressurized atmosphere.

It is a pity that the only equivalent place in Britain's High Streets appears to be the betting shop. The emergence of independent financial advisers should have led to the development of money shops, but not very many exist. For the most part the advisers stick to insurance broking, leaving share dealing to the banks and big securities houses.

12 Policing the Markets

'The financial planning industry is in many ways still in the days of the Wild West. The marshal hasn't ridden into town, there's mayhem in the streets, a lot of random shooting.' – Scott Stapf of the North American Securities Administrators' Association.

At four o'clock in the morning of October 23, 1812, three men called at the Popincourt Barracks in Paris with the devastating news that the Emperor Napoleon had died beneath the walls of Moscow. It was a plausible story – news from the campaign front took three weeks to get back and the French armies had just achieved a great victory at the Battle of Borodino that had opened the gates to the Russian capital. The men also said that the Senate had abolished the Empire and appointed a Provisional Government, and was calling on the 10th Cohort of the National Guard for support. Within hours a huge conspiracy against Napoleon was under way, and the Emperor's leading supporters were thrown into prison.

This story, told in more recent times by Italian author, Guido Artom, in his book *Napoleon is Dead in Russia*, was the inspiration for one of Britain's most notorious examples of share market rigging. In the early nineteenth century only major news moved the fledgling Stock Market, and it took headlines like 'Napoleon set to Invade', or, better still, 'Napoleon Dead' to move the market.

Since, even in the days before the telegraph, old news was no news, stockbrokers often placed faithful retainers in the port of Dover to listen to the rumour mill, watch the sea, talk to fishermen, and report back regularly. So, when on February 21, 1814, Colonel de Burgh, alias Charles Random de Bérenger, turned up in Dover in a red uniform, saying he was aide de camp to General Lord Cathcart, and reported the death of Napoleon and the fall of Paris, the news flashed to London at the speed of a pony and trap. Although foreign reporting was severely limited in those days, along with share ownership, there were those in London who had heard of the earlier, unsuccessful conspiracy against Napoleon, and the subsequent execution, not only of the plotters, but also of the soldiers who unwittingly carried the message. They were therefore very much on their guard against such embellishments. But 'Colonel de Burgh' had an elaborate story, a detailed account of how Napoleon had been butchered by the Cossacks. He had also made a point of going directly to the headquarters of the Port Admiral in Dover to apprise him of the facts. Surely, said brokers, it must be true.

Prices on the Stock Exchange shot up, as the wealthy clients of brokers received the news, apparently confirmed by hand bills distributed in the streets of London. They were not to know that these had also been handed out by de Bérenger who had himself taken a coach to the capital, to collect his gains, estimated at about £10,000. It was, of course, all pure fraud, but note that those who lost out were those who had been contacted by brokers, those who, themselves, were privileged possessors of inside information, which, in this case, turned out to be false.

Not much changed in the following 175 years. Until recently it was those 'in the know' who stood to make rich pickings from speculative trading on the Stock Exchange. Latter-day frauds on similar lines to that perpetrated by de Bérenger were common in the early 1970s, during the so-called Australian mining boom. Reports of a nickel 'strike' by an obscure, barely known and usually recently listed mining company would reach Sydney as a result of a tip from Kalgoorlie, a remote dusty gold town in Western Australia. Confirmation was impossible, but the word flashed round, and the price of the stock shot up. I once worked on a magazine where the financial editor would return from lunch, very excited, and shout something like 'Bosom's Creek has struck nickel', and rush to the phone to buy shares. Some brokers made a point of reserving shares for journalists, who could be counted upon to write favourably about a mining prospect, which, more often than not, when the geologists' reports arrived, turned out to be nothing more than a hole in the ground or a stick marking a spot in the desert. Fortunes were made and lost. An old friend, the secretary to a prominent Australian politician, made over £100,000 from share trading in Poseidon.

Much of the activity was 12,000 miles from the geologists' trowels. Each day, as soon as the London Stock Exchange opened there was feverish activity as investors sought to cash in. Many had their fingers badly burned, and the two year 'boom' earned Australian brokers a bad reputation which they have only recently lived down. As one merchant banker, who frequently visits Sydney, put it: 'The Aussies saw it as a way of getting their own back on the Poms'.

Ramping stocks was not confined to those on the fringe of share markets. Writing in *The Observer* on September 5 1971, under the headline 'Digging up the Dirt', I reported how an Australian Senate Committee investigation into the series of mining collapses and false claims in that country had severely shaken investors' confidence.

One thoroughly dishonest practice disclosed to the Committee was the purchase of huge blocks of shares in early trading by certain brokers, using their house accounts. By lunchtime, word would be round the markets that a particular share was on the move, and the broking house would unload its newly acquired holding at a substantial profit. Those shares that remained unsold would be allocated to clients for whom the firm held discretionary accounts, at a substantially higher price than the firm had paid for them, thereby enabling it to take a profit at its clients' expense. To add insult to injury, the clients would be charged brokerage, but usually would be none the wiser, for they would see from the *Australian Financial Review* that they had apparently obtained the shares at the 'market price'.

The Committee's report makes interesting reading, even years after the inquiry. It scrutinized in detail the accounts of one sharebroking firm that had gone into liquidation, only to find that about 80 per cent of the firm's trading was on its own account, and that its income from commission amounted to only a minor proportion of turnover.

Another prominent Sydney stockbroker, who was also a director of two major mining companies, was exposed for trying to have one of the companies taken over by a joint venture operation, in which his stockbroking firm's affiliated investment house had a stake. Evidence to the Senate Committee revealed that the stockbroker planned the takeover without informing the company chairman or his fellow directors, and that an associate company of his firm was to act as the underwriters.

Let us move back to London, and to June 13 1985. It was a typical summer Thursday on the Stock Exchange. Trading was languid, as is so often the case at this time of the year. Then came a sudden burst of activity, much to the curiosity of a party from a Norfolk Women's Institute that was visiting the public gallery that day. Someone was buying large blocks of shares in Arthur Bell and Sons plc, and their prices rose by 14 per cent.

The visitors had to wait until reading their Saturday edition of the *Eastern Daily Press* to find out why. Guinness plc had made a bid for Bell on Friday the 14th, and on the eve of that takeover offer, someone had got wind of what was going on, and had been buying Bell's shares furiously in the hope of a quick profit. Yet 'insider trading' is strictly forbidden both by the law, which since 1980 has made it a criminal offence, and by the rules of the Stock Exchange. Despite that, as a practice, it is rife.

According to Philip Healey, editor of the magazine *Acquisitions Monthly*, the share prices of takeover targets rise on average between 20 and 30 per cent in the month before a bid. Over 90 per cent of prices move before a bid. One reason for this may well be that astute investors have spotted, from their own research, likely targets for takeover.

But, that apart, the Stock Exchange says that in recent years it logged more than 2,000 suspicious price movements a month, and referred some of the worst cases to the Department of Trade and Industry.

The Stock Exchange maintains a special squad of men and women at its Throgmorton Street offices to try to track down insider traders. This means questioning those suspected of using inside knowledge to make money, and putting the evidence before the Exchange's Disciplinary Committee.

New and powerful computers allow the squad to spot erratic price movements in London and on other major international markets, and they have the authority to question anyone who works for a member of the Stock Exchange, which, of course, includes a large number of international banks and other financial conglomerates. Their computers have instant access to all Stock Exchange transactions over the previous six months, and they may manipulate the data base by asking over 100 questions.

But just like detectives from the regular police forces, they rely more on hot tips from informants than from the craftsmanship of a Sherlock Holmes. The number of tips runs at about ten a week. Many of them come from market-makers in the City using the SEAQ terminals, and spotting something suspicious. Since market-makers can lose thousands of pounds by incorrect pricing, they are very aware of phoney figures.

They also have the backing of compliance officers employed in securities houses. These men and women make sure that both the Stock Exchange rules and their own house rules on share trading are strictly observed, and if they spot an irregularity in a transaction involving another firm, they usually report it to their opposite number.

Some companies are stricter than others in observing the code of conduct they insist staff must obey when buying and selling stock on their own account. Chase Securities insists that all transactions are placed through the company, and that compliance staff are notified. At Barclays de Zoete Wedd, the phone transactions of all dealing staff are logged, so that investigators could, if they wished, find out who telephone whom and when. Some firms have taken this a stage further and record all telephone calls.

A mixture of recorded conversations and the alertness of the London Stock Exchange's surveillance unit has already been responsible for trapping several insider traders. Just before the Mecca group bid for Pleasurama, the casinos and restaurant company, the members of the unit spotted that there had been an increasing amount of trading in Pleasurama. Their suspicions were further aroused when they received calls from market-makers in some leading broking firms drawing their attention to the fact that something irregular must be going on. Compliance officers at several houses were phoned, and after a tape at Morgan Grenfell had been played, it was discovered that a tip had been passed on by a female member of Samuel Montagu's corporate finance team. This was the department involved in advising Mecca on its offer. The other banks then listened to their own tape recordings, and the woman plus two others who had used the information were unceremoniously sacked. The three stood to have made a useful sum of money from trading on inside information. That they were caught owes much to their own greed and the vigilance of the surveillance squad. If they had been more cautious and less avaricious their dealings might well have passed unnoticed.

Even so, many insider traders escape detection. One particular problem is the use of nominee companies in offshore tax havens as the trading vehicle. The head of the Stock Exchange squad, Mike Feltham, and his team of former policemen, computer consultants, stockbrokers and accountants, say they often follow good leads only to come up against obstacles when a block of shares is purchased by a nominee company. 'There is no way we can see at the moment of busting offshore companies without international cooperation', Feltham told me: 'All the old names are always there – the Cayman Isles and so on. But it is not only in the Caribbean or in Liberia that this problem exists – much closer to home, in the Channel Isles or the Isle of Man we have just no hope of getting behind the nominee thing.

'Another big problem is that when we want to interview someone who has dealt in the market, we have absolutely no power to go and talk to that person unless he or his firm is a member of the Exchange. In America, for instance, it is very different. An investigator can get a subpoena more or less immediately.'

Up Before The Courts

The Magistrates' Court at Bow Street just off the Strand in Central London has seen more villains pass through its doors than most. The majority do not tarry for long. They plead guilty, are fined a nominal amount, and vanish into the street to repeat the petty offences with which they have been charged, sparing hardly a glance at the gleaming cream stucco of the Royal Opera House opposite. The clientele are usually prostitutes, pickpockets, petty criminals and shop-lifters.

But on November 3 1987 there was an unusually large number of cameramen and journalists jostling on the pavement outside the railings of the court. And there were some unusual defendants – Ernest Saunders, former chairman and chief executive of one of Britain's most famous breweries, Guinness; Roger Seelig, the former corporate finance director of Morgan Grenfell, one of Britain's blue blood merchant banks, and Sir Jack Lyons, a businessman. They, together with Anthony Parnes, a stockbroker, and Gerald Ronson, head of the Heron garages and petrol group, were all charged with fraud in connection with what was to become known as the Guinness affair.

Saunders faced 40 charges, Sir Jack 9, and Seelig 12. In each case the charges involved alleged theft from Guinness. Some of the charges related to the actions of those accused during the successful takeover by Guinness of Bell, the Scottish whisky company, mentioned earlier. It is not the purpose of this book to delve into a case history that has become as thick and impenetrable as the Guinness brew. All were found guilty on a number of the charges, and were sent to prison.

Policing the markets is conducted in two ways: through self-regulation by quasi-official bodies set up by stock exchanges in consultation with governments, or by official agencies staffed by professionals. For many years there have been arguments about which is the more effective way of protecting the investor and preventing fraud and corruption. The debate continues, but, with time and experience, the weight of opinion seems to be moving in favour of a regulatory system run by full-time professionals with no vested interest in any company within the securities industry.

The most important regulatory body in the world is the United States Securities and Exchange Commission (SEC), which protects the interests of America's estimated 50 million investors. Although its authority is technically limited to policing the securities industry in the United States, its tentacles are spread much wider, extending, for example, to the conduct of American investment institutions in their operations outside the country.

The SEC, with a staff of 1,800, was established in July

1935, some years after the Wall Street crash of 1929. A Congressional investigation found that there had been stock manipulation on a huge scale, blatant dishonesty and insider trading, and the SEC was established with sweeping powers over the securities industry.

Now all corporations have to file quarterly financial returns, and much more detailed annual ones, with the SEC, as well as informing it promptly of any facts or important events which might affect the market for the company's stock. Federal laws require companies intending to raise money by selling their own securities to file with the Commission true facts about their operations. The Commission has power to prevent or punish fraud in the sale of securities, and is authorized to regulate stock exchanges. The law under which it operates lays down precise boundaries within which directors, officers and large shareholders may deal in the stock of their companies.

In its time the SEC has notched up some notable successes in prosecuting corporate crime. In August 1968, it filed charges of securities fraud against 14 Merrill Lynch officers and employees. In the end Merrill Lynch publicly consented to an SEC finding that it had used advance inside information from the Douglas Aircraft Company for the advantage of preferred institutional clients, defrauding the investing public of an estimated $4.5m. in the process – no mean sum at the time. Unlike the British Department of Trade and Industry, the Securities and Exchange Commission is a mecca for bright young lawyers who wish to make their name as determined investigators, and then, as often as not, get out into lucrative private practice with the SEC name on their credentials. Just after the SEC netted Dennis Levine, a senior executive of Drexel Burnham Lambert, for insider trading, in the spring of 1986, I flew to New York to look at how the organization worked. Was it really more efficient than the self-regulation the City favoured? One was immediately struck by the professional approach of the organization, and the determination of its officers to pin down the crooks.

However, while the SEC has a reputation as a vigorous force, and has notched up a number of successes (the most notable of which was the successful prosecution of insider trader Ivan Boesky mentioned earlier) it is severely constrained in its activities by a shortage of funds. Although the SEC collects fees from registered investment advisers, it has to hand over a large share of the proceeds to the United States Treasury. It has only 314 enforcement officers to cover the whole of the United States, and the section which deals with the investment management and mutual funds industry has an inspectorate of only about 60 people.

Although this group undertakes about 1,500 spot checks each year on investment advisers, it is not surprising that many confidence tricksters escape unscathed. Officially there are about 16,500 registered investment advisers in the United States, so on average each gets a spot check once a decade, during which time many will have sold their businesses on. But these figures include only the registered advisers. The Consumer Federation of America (CFA) believes that there could be about half a million people acting as unofficial financial advisers, while even the Securities Administrators Association accepts that there are 250,000. Many of these not only claim to offer investment advice; some of them actually manage clients' money.

The CFA gave me some alarming figures. In 1990 it believed that investment advisers handle more than a quarter of the entire nation's savings, a sum exceeding $4,000 billion. It claims that $1 billion a year is lost through fraud. That may seem a small percentage – compared with, say, credit card fraud – but considering the fact that it is almost always private individuals with small savings who suffer, it is a matter of considerable public concern.

Many of these frauds are simple scams. For example, 400 investors on the West Coast lost $7 million when they put their money into a fund run by a financial adviser who promised them a return of between 30 and 40 per cent in trading by a bank in Certificates of Deposit, precious metals and international arbitrage. The 'bank', in the Marshall Islands, a US protectorate, turned out to be a gas station, whose owner merely went to the post office and re-mailed the incoming cheques to the financial adviser. Unusually, in this case, the scam was uncovered before the financial adviser and his collaborator vanished.

The SEC also depends greatly on a number of self-regulatory bodies to fulfil its task. For the most part stock exchanges police the activities of their members, and each has an investigations branch. The New York Stock Exchange, the American Stock Exchange and the National Association of Securities Dealers (NASDAQ) all work in close cooperation with the SEC.

The SEC has much wider powers than the Department of Trade, and has much more inclination to use them. The DTI so far has been reluctant to use its power to force open bank accounts and to demand documents, though this may change. But the SEC may subpoena individuals and companies in the US, and demand sight of their bank accounts. Outside America it has agreements with the British, Japanese, Swiss, Cayman Isles and other governments to gather information, and it can also call for sanctions to be imposed on the US branches of un-cooperative foreign banks. Offenders may not only be prosecuted, with penalties as high as three times the illicit profits, but the SEC will turn over all the evidence it has gained to civil litigants who have been disadvantaged as a result of someone's insider trading.

Even these powers are inadequate when one considers the definition of the modus operandi of an insider trader provided by the *Financial Times*:

> The would-be insider trader gets a job with the corporate finance department of a merchant bank active in mergers and acquisitions. Always travelling via a third country, he visits two tax havens, Panama and Liechtenstein, which have resisted foreign pressure on their secrecy laws. In each company he sets up a trading company, and opens bank accounts in two or three banks in their names. He only uses banks with no operations or assets in Britain or the United States. He never tells the banks his real name, but arranges for them to deal through a large London broking firm whenever they receive coded instructions over the telephone.
>
> When he picks up inside information, he always trades alone using a call box. He never trades in large amounts, but may break up a transaction into a series of deals from different accounts. He avoids the mistake of trading just before a bid announcement – it makes the market makers vengeful.

As the *Financial Times* pointed out, the SEC's achievements highlighted 'the passivity of the DTI'.

Curiously, though, it was the SEC's biggest coup, catching Ivan F. Boesky, the self-styled 'king of the arbs', that provided the DTI with some of their best leads into City fraud this side of the Atlantic.

Boesky was brought to book because of the Levine case mentioned earlier. Levine pleaded guilty, paid back $12.6m. in illegal profits, and sang like a canary to the SEC, implicating Boesky. Boesky was charged with making a personal killing on insider information provided by Levine, fined $100m. dollars, barred for life from working on Wall Street, and ordered to dismantle his $2bn. firm.

Boesky was one of the biggest and best known speculators in the feverish takeover business in America, using a phenomenal network of contacts to make huge profits through arbitraging. Like Levine, he also 'cooperated with the authorities', which is a euphemism for becoming a supergrass in order to keep out of jail.

The Gower Report

The British decided against establishing a SEC and in favour of self-regulation after commissioning a three-year study by Professor Jim Gower.

In his report, which provides the foundation for the Financial Services Act, Professor Gower found that criticism in City circles of the SEC as a 'mammoth, lawyer-dominated, over-regulatory bureaucracy' was greatly exaggerated, but nevertheless he shrank from recommending the establishment of 'anything so elaborate'.

Undoubtedly he was swayed by the old maxim that 'politics is the art of the possible', for he declared:

> such a recommendation would clearly not be accepted by the present Government which dislikes quangos. While it would have influential supporters among the Labour Party, it too has always failed to establish a Securities Commission when in power – under less unfavourable economic conditions than at present. I do not imagine that the Liberal-SDP Alliance would be any more enthusiastic about facing a head-on collision with the City establishment. For I have been left in no doubt of the City's rooted objection to a Commission.

Professor Gower also pointed out that the American example was seen as part of the Roosevelt New Deal, and thereby attracted to its staff some of the most able and idealistic products of the universities and law schools. A British body in the 1980s would not, he felt, have similar appeal. And in recommending the course that the Government was later to adopt – the delegation of new and tougher regulations to bodies like the Stock Exchange – Professor Gower unearthed a quotation from one of the founding fathers of the US SEC indicating his belief in the ideal of having a self-regulatory organization:

> so organized and so imbued with the public interest that it would be possible and even desirable to entrust to them a great deal of the actual regulation and enforcement within their own field, leaving the Government free to pursue a supervisory or residual role.

Gower added, wryly:

> In the United States that ideal was not achieved, partly because in 1938 it was dramatically revealed that the leading self-regulatory agency, the New York Stock Exchange, could not then be regarded as sufficiently 'imbued with the public interest'.

The New Regulators

The British Government's response to the Gower report and the lobbying that accompanied and followed its publication was to come up with a classic Whitehall fudge. Essentially the City would be left to police itself. But because it could not be trusted to do so, a Securities and Investment Board was established, staffed by professionals and headed by Sir Kenneth Berrill, a distinguished public servant who had once led the Central Policy Review Staff. The SIB would sit on top of a plethora of self-regulatory bodies – one of which would be the Stock Exchange – and would make sure they did their stuff. Tougher new rule books would have to be drawn up, approved and enforced. And just to make sure that Westminster still held the whip hand, the DTI would remain as the final arbiter.

The SIB is an unusual animal. It wields widespread regulatory powers, ranging from the right to take investment businesses to court to obtain restitution for clients, to conducting criminal prosecutions. But it is financed entirely by the financial markets themselves, with no contribution from the Exchequer.

Once installed, Sir Kenneth set about his task like a man possessed. His brief was the Financial Services Act, an ambitious piece of legislation that had been rushed through Parliament without sufficient thought having been given to its impact on the City or investors. His mandate was to license all those who ran investment businesses, from the blue-chip insurance companies and the blue-blooded stockbrokers to the local bank manager and mortgage broker. None would escape the net – and by the summer of 1988, 40,000 companies or individuals had been authorized, and a number of others had been forced to shut down.

A dozen or so self-regulatory bodies had also been established. One is The Securities Association (TSA), which took over the regulatory role of the Stock Exchange. Others were LAUTRO, the Life Assurance and Unit Trust Regulatory Organization, composed of companies offering savings and investment products and services; the Association of Futures Brokers and Dealers (AFBD); and the Investment Management Regulatory Organization (IMRO). Perhaps the most prominent and controversial is the Financial Intermediaries, Managers and Brokers Regulatory Association, FIMBRA, whose membership is mainly insurance brokers and financial advisers, who had previously been among the most criticized groups, partly because they were remunerated almost entirely by commission.

Other self-regulatory bodies included the Law Society and the Association of Chartered Accountants, whose governing bodies have determined if, how and when their members should provide financial advisory services.

The SIB and these bodies had to follow a number of guidelines laid down by the Financial Services Act. Approved investment businesses had to be competent, financially sound, and offer 'best advice' after 'getting to know' the customer.

Sir Kenneth had two choices. He could leave the definitions

vague, and trust the self-regulatory bodies to interpret the law in a reasonable way, or he could draw up very detailed rules so that there could be no ambiguity about what was and was not permissible. He chose the latter, and as a result those practising in the financial services industry have to face some of the most perplexing, extensive, expensive and taxing conditions imposed on any sector of industry anywhere. Whereas the American Declaration of Independence ran to only 1,337 words – and the Ten Commandments to a mere 333 words – the SIB and SRO rulebooks run to more than a million words. Some of the rules have changed the way major institutions do business. A stockbroker can no longer call a client and suggest he buys a share – this falls foul of rules on cold-calling, aimed primarily at high pressure salesmen who used to make a practice of knocking on the doors of the recently-bereaved in order to talk their way into some new business. Ironically life salesmen – the worst offenders – are exempt from the general prohibition on cold-calling, although the customer now has a 14–day cooling off period during which he is able to rescind the transaction if he wishes.

Financial advisers, including stockbrokers, have to observe the 'know your customer' rule. This means they must take reasonable steps to find out about the financial circumstances of clients and advise them accordingly. This responsibility is reduced if the client is deemed an 'experienced investor' with a clear understanding of risk.

There is also a 'best execution' rule. There is no question of buying for yourself first and the client later, if prices are rising. A broker must strike a deal on the best terms available – and must keep records which may be matched to computer records to establish whether deals were concluded in good time and at the best prices.

Authorized firms are required to have proper in-house procedures for investigating customers' complaints. If a client is not happy with this, he may approach the self-regulatory organization or the Securities and Investments Board itself. Any institution – whether it be a bank, building society or insurance company – also faces the rule of polarization, one of the most controversial of Sir Kenneth's innovations. This states that an organization may offer, through its branch network, either its own range of policies and investment products or everyone else's – but not both. The idea of the rule is to prevent a conflict of interest occurring when a bank or building society manager offers his customers investment advice. If he were able to offer a total service, so the SIB argument goes, he would give preference to his own company's products even when they offered inferior terms or performance. So, for example, at the time of writing, managers of Barclays, Lloyds and Midland banks can only advise customers on life, endowment, pensions and PEP schemes provided by themselves or their subsidiaries. If an account holder sees an advertisement on television for a Norwich Union endowment scheme or a Scottish Mutual pension – and goes, as the commercial suggests, to see his financial adviser, in the shape of a Barclays, Lloyds or Midland bank manager, the manager must tell him he is not allowed to enter into a discussion. Should he bank with the National Westminster or the Bank of Scotland, however, the manager will give him a warm welcome, until the customer asks about the bank's own products, in which case he will dry up.

The polarized banks have managed to circumvent the SIB rules, however, by establishing independent insurance brokerages which operate at regional level. So the person inquiring about the Norwich Union TV commercial will be invited to contact Barclays' Insurance Services, which, provided the inquirer requests it, will send out a special representative to see him. It is a far cry from the days when bank managers added substantially to their remuneration by earning commission from selling insurance. Because of the new restrictions, which do not apply to direct investment in shares or gilts, the bank manager is much more likely these days to steer his clients into a high-interest deposit account, or, most probable of all, a bigger mortgage. Sir Kenneth's extraordinary determination – coupled with the all-embracing nature of his SIB network – eventually caused him to part company with the City, and he has now retired. A former Bank of England executive, David Walker, took over, and has made rules less onerous and more intelligible.

Disclosing Commission
Life assurance is sold not bought, the adage goes. This concept has been used for decades to justify the belief that most

families in Britain would not be prepared to pay fees for investment advice, and would therefore be inclined to put their savings into a building society, bank or shares rather than into a long-term plan built around a life policy. So insurance brokers and other financial advisers have earned a comfortable living from commission based on the premiums of the policies they have sold. In most cases the bulk of the commission has been paid immediately upon acceptance of the contract, thus often effectively handing over the first year's premium to the intermediary.

Few of those taking out such policies – and particularly long-term endowment plans in support of a big mortgage – had any idea how much money was being paid out in commission or other expenses. For this reason, few questioned whether the advice they were receiving was impartial. A financial adviser was hardly likely to recommend a client to buy gilts or the shares of blue chip companies when he derived no benefit from such a recommendation. For a while even the SIB allowed itself to be blinded by the 'sold not bought' argument. With an unusually large proportion of its members coming from the life assurance industry – and with its deputy chairman, Sir Mark Weinberg, the head of a company known for its salesmanship skills – it was perhaps not surprising, but disgraceful nevertheless, that the SIB accepted a proposal from LAUTRO that there should be 'soft disclosure' of commissions by independent brokers. 'Soft disclosure' of course, was a euphemism for pulling the wool over the eyes of the public: what it meant was that brokers would tell clients that commission was based on the normal agreed scale, without stating what that scale was.

This purblind arrangement came to the attention of the hawk-eyed Sir Gordon Borrie, director of the Office of Fair Trading, when he was scrutinizing the LAUTRO rulebook. He recommended an insistance on hard disclosure. After several weeks of negotiations in 1988, in which the DTI threatened not to accept the rulebook, LAUTRO finally accepted a compromise that the details of commissions would have to be disclosed. But even now it is something which is only in the small print.

Market-rigging

The issue of commission disclosure caused no problems for stockbrokers, who were in the process of reducing charges for those institutions trading in large volumes while increasing dealing rates for the small private investor. Securities houses had other worries. The law relating to information in a prospectus was made more onerous. The basic requirement is that listing particulars must contain all the information that investors and their professional advisers could reasonably require to be able to make an informed assessments of the assets and liabilities, financial position, profits and losses and prospects of the issuer of securities. The law on misleading statements was made tougher. The Financial Services Act made it an offence to create a 'false or misleading impression as to the market in or the price or value of any investments' if this was done with the purpose of inducing an investment transaction. Thus the common practice of hyping shares became illegal, even if the Government had been guilty of doing so itself in the early privatizations. All published recommendations in analysts' reports must be researched and capable of substantiation – the stockbroker's 'hunch' is out.

Advertisements, too, must be fair, accurate and complete. The severity of the application of this rule varies according to the form of advertisement – the simplest requirement being for those advertisements which convey little or no message, and the most stringent for advertisements asking readings to cut-out and post a coupon together with money. Here the rules require fair and complete disclosure of relevant facts, and the substantiation of all statements of fact. Investment advertisements, including mailshots, must contain a 'health' warning about matters such as the volatility or the marketability of the product advertised. Only authorized businesses can place investment advertisements, and publishers have an obligation to check the SIB lists. If an advertisement is deemed to be an investment advertisement, it must be approved by a firm authorized under the Financial Services Act. But most British industrial companies are not, and their half-yearly and annual results advertisements are deemed, in many cases, to be persuading shareholders that an investment in the organization is a good thing. So they must have the advertisement checked and placed by a firm that is authorized: either stockbrokers, accountants or solicitors.

Large groups which act both as investment advisers to the public or corporations also working as investment bankers to raise the capital, have to establish so-called Chinese Walls inside their firms to prevent one department acting on privileged information available to another.

Any of the new financial conglomerates has the power to act simultaneously as banker to a company, raise long-term debt or equity, make a market in the securities involved, retail them to investors, and buy them as managers of discretionary funds. The object is to establish a barrier of silence and confidentiality between those carrying out these tasks, so that they do not enjoy advantages not shared by competitors, or the investing public.

The theory of Chinese Walls is that John Smith, involved either in raising funds for a company or organizing a disposal, will not seek to influence Peter Brown, in the fund management department, either by seeking his support in a purchase, or tipping him off about a possible sale. It is a good theory, dependent 100 per cent on the integrity of everyone involved, but it is inconsistent with all the standards imposed on those who face conflicts of interest in other areas of commerce, politics and local government. One definition of the practice runs as follows:

> A Chinese Wall is an established arrangement whereby information known to a person in one part of the business is not available, directly or indirectly, to those involved in another part of a business, and it is accepted that in each of the parts of the business so divided decisions will be taken without reference to any interest which any other such part or any person in such part of the business may have in the matter.

To help physically to create Chinese Walls, some companies have actually separated functions into different City buildings, often half a mile apart. For example, Hill Samuel and Co Ltd, merchant bankers, occupy offices in Wood Street, just opposite the headquarters of the City Fraud Squad to the south of the Barbican development, while Hill Samuel Investment Management is on the north side of the Barbican, in Beech Street. Lazards operate their own Chinese Walls within narrower confines. Overlooking a drab concrete square on Moorfield Highwalk is Lazard Brothers and Co Ltd, the merchant bank. Thirty yards away, on the adjacent side of the square, and separated only by a pedestrian walkway, is Lazard Securities Ltd, the fund management arm of the company. Equidistant from both is a large and well-patronized wine bar and hostelry, the 'City Boot' – exactly where the Chinese Wall is supposed to be. Both at lunchtime and in the early evening it is packed with Lazards' men, not the clerks and typists, but the middle-rank officers of both companies.

The Barlow Clowes Affair

In the summer of 1988, there emerged another major scandal which tested the effectiveness of the new investor protection regime to the full – the Barlow Clowes Affair. Thousands of investors suddenly discovered from reading their daily papers that the money they had set aside for pension or other long-term savings by investing in a number of funds run by a Cheshire-based group, Barlow Clowes, had vanished, and that the firm had been put into liquidation. This may be a familiar tale in the history of personal investment, but what made matters worse was that most of the funds lost were commuted lump sums from life savings or pensions and redundancy payments. A majority of the investors were elderly.

What was also particularly interesting about this scandal was that it embroiled both financial advisers and the government. It was not just a case of investors losing their savings as a result of sharp practice by a fund management group. Many of the 11,000 who lost a major part of their life savings did so after being advised to invest in the Barlow Clowes fund by professional independent financial advisers – one of whom was a high profile lady on the board of one of the self-regulatory bodies, FIMBRA – who could have been presumed to have known better. Their defence was that Barlow Clowes had actually been licensed by the Department of Trade and Industry, *after* suspicions had been raised about the firm's activities.

Barlow Clowes, like many other similar funds, was built up as a low-cost fund management group. Its funds were certainly not designed to attract the reckless; indeed its very appeal was to the cautious investor who wanted to avoid the risks inherent in equities but who sought a better return than that available from a bank or building society deposit. The attraction was that expert managers would consolidate investors' cash into interest-bearing deposits, principally British gilt-edged securities.

Gilt or bond funds are quite common. Most of the well established fund management groups successfully operate them. Their return on funds invested is usually solid rather than exciting – but in the period that immediately followed the October 1987 crash they provided the reassuring promise of preserving a nest-egg. For example, in the summer of 1988 when Barlow Clowes investors learned that the Securities and Investment Board had acted to put the company into liquidation, most of the gilts funds were riding high. Had investors put their money into the Royal Trust Preference Fund, for instance, they would have had a profit of £350 for every £1,000 invested. Funds run by other companies such as Gartmore, Target and Henderson were all showing a return well in excess of bank or building society 'high-interest' deposits.

The reader may well ask why those seeking risk-averse investment opportunities should put their savings into Barlow Clowes? The answer, of course, is marketing. The Barlow Clowes funds were heavily advertised as foolproof. Investors were told that their money was 'as safe as in the Bank of England'. Another reason is that many financial advisers were picking up above-average commissions for placing their clients' funds into the funds – illegally under the 'best advice' rules, which, of course, were not in place when many of the recommendations were made. Some advisers were later suspended. One Cheshire firm, a member of the professional British Insurance and Investment Brokers Association, was suspended by FIMBRA after it was revealed that it had taken 2 per cent of invested funds in commission and its principal had been on trips to Gibralter with Peter Clowes.

Inevitably, once liquidators were appointed, it was quickly discovered that much of the money entrusted to Barlow Clowes did not find its way into gilt-edged securities, as the managers had promised. Although officials of Spicer and Oppenheim hunted across Europe in an attempt to find the Barlow Clowes money, only a proportion of the 'safe' investments was recovered, and many people lost their savings. Early on it was discovered that a clause in the investment contract, not brought to the attention of clients by their financial advisers, permitted the fund managers to place the monies anywhere they thought fit, which is undoubtedly what they did, enriching their own lifestyles along the way. It was also revealed that Barlow Clowes had lent large sums of money to companies in which its principal, Peter Clowes, had an interest.

Investors in the British part of Barlow Clowes eventually received much of their money back, but those who ventured into the Gibralter-based offshore funds lost most of their investments, and faced the threat of a bill from the Inland Revenue for the tax they had not paid on the annual dividends which had been ploughed back into the company.

It was a sorry tale, and it showed up all the weaknesses of the Financial Services Act, although it must be said that but for the vigilance of the Securities and Investment Board, the operation might have continued for some time, its activities cloaked under a façade of marketing misinformation.

Unfortunately for the hapless investors in Barlow Clowes, they lost their money before the establishment of the Securities and Investment Board's compensation scheme, which was supposed to have been in place at the same time as the FSA became effective but whose introduction was delayed until August 1988. Once again the scheme was a victory for the lobbyists from the life assurance movement – the companies were exempted from making a contribution to the cost, as were the building societies. The large clearing banks claimed they would be shouldering an unfair burden of the cost of rescuing investors in firms taking much greater risks. 'Why should the strong and the good bail out the others?' asked Natwest's Lord Boardman, with reason.

The scheme started with a maximum of £48,000 of compensation to anyone suffering from a default, and cost all investment firms an average of one per cent of their gross revenues. Within a year of its establishment the new regulatory framework had raised standards and reduced the chances of the investor being taken for a ride. It had established the first register of investment practitioners in Britain, and the first rulebook governing their activities. But all this was achieved at a cost, which ultimately had to be paid for by the investor. The impact of regulation is also likely to drive more investors into the hands of the large institutions, which, as we shall see later, has its own dangers.

The Barlow Clowes affair, the Guinness prosecutions, and a number of other frauds made the British government stiffen the role of the Securities and Investments Board. At the same time it made it more palatable to City institutions by appointing the Bank of England's David Walker as its chairman.

The complaint had been that there had been over-regulation: Walker's response was to rewrite the rule books, and reduce the number of self-regulatory organizations from five to four by merging the Securities Association and the Association of Futures Brokers into one organization. John Young, chairman of the merged body, the SFA, said: 'Our job is to make regulation simple and cheating difficult'.

I cannot help feeling that the Financial Services Act in Britain created a monster which is still out of control, and achieves little for the ordinary investor. According to the *Daily Telegraph* in August 1991 the bureaucracy created by the act costs more than £1.25 million a week, equivalent to £130 a year for every personal equity plan investor. This bill covers only the direct costs of the five regulatory bodies.

My own view is that the focus needs to be narrowed further. Perhaps only two regulatory bodies are needed – one for the retail sector, licensing financial advisers and setting very tough rules for their operations; and the other for the international professionals. For the latter it is hard to escape the view that a Pan-European body, modelled on the lines of the United States SEC, would be the best solution.

For the former the regulatory body needs to provide some consumer education. Research published in 1991 by Mintel

showed that despite £424 millions worth of financial advertising the previous year, the majority of the population did
not know what it was buying. Only ten per cent of those
questioned said they were influenced by an independent
adviser. No wonder the SIB published a booklet, *How to
Spot the Investment Cowboy*, which contained the
memorable phrase: 'Having been wary, you should continue
to be so when you have parted with your money'.

13 Beyond Babel

'There is nothing more difficult to take in hand, more perilous to conduct, more certain in its success, than to take the lead in introducing a new order of things; because the innovator will have for enemies all who have done well under the old conditions and only lukewarm defenders in those who may do well under the new.' – Machiavelli, The Prince.

In Britain most people's image of the stock market is conjured up by the television news pictures of aggressive but washed-out dealers staring at TV screens and shouting down the telephone at each other. Movies like *Wall Street* and TV series like *Capital City* depict the market-place of international finance as a crazed indoor version of the bookmakers' enclosure at a racetrack. Few British people have any notion of this being a place where funds are raised to develop industry and to create jobs, or where their pension contributions are invested for their old age.

In a revealing study published in 1990 the London Stock Exchange said it had found that most people distrusted stockbrokers, thinking of them 'either as arrogant, upper-crust old Etonian types, or youthful wheeler-dealers in the model of an estate agent'.

For this we have only the City of London to blame. It tends toward arrogance. It never pauses for breath long enough to explain its role in the British or world economy in terms that ordinary people can understand. Its public relations are appalling. Those in the City employed in marketing seem interested only in packaging life assurance policies and unit trusts through sales methods more suited to double-glazing than investments.

Yet my experience is that thousands of decent people come into the Square Mile each day to work towards the common goal of creating an efficient financial centre, competing for business, looking for new opportunities in which to invest the funds entrusted to their care.

The trouble is that the City lacks leadership. The babel created by new technology has overturned one centuries-old system, but has left the City – and many of its institutions – unsure of which direction they are headed.

In the 1980s the clubbish world of the London Stock Exchange was turned upside down. There is no longer a busy paper-strewn trading floor, no noisy flurry of activity for visitors to watch, no bells ringing for the opening or the close. The exchange itself is no more; the people in the building in Throgmorton Street Stcok Exchange are mostly concerned with regulation, compliance, settlements and power struggles.

The markets have no epicentre, for deals are struck in the ether between satellite dishes, telephones and computer terminals. The exchange still retains the motto: 'My Word is My Bond', but deals are recorded on tape, a sign of the times and just in case there is misunderstanding.

Competition has intensified. Many of the famous old broking firms no longer want to deal with the general public, and a number of houses have been losing money. Many famous names have gone forever. The institutions have been able to buy and sell shares cheaper, but most of us have paid more, denying the boast of the Stock Exchange pre-Big Bang that investors as a whole would gain. Within two years of the abolition of fixed commissions the charge per transaction by the majority of houses was £20 or more, although commission rates remained the same: 1.65 per cent on the first £7,000; 0.5 per cent or thereabouts for larger bargains. Almost as important as commissions has been the widening of the spread between buying and selling prices. The market-makers on their electronic terminals are taking much less of a risk than the old-fashioned jobbers. Before Big Bang the jobber's turn was on average 1.2 per cent. By the end of 1990 the gap was 2 per cent. On unit trusts the gap between bid and offer was even wider, sometimes 5 per cent or more. The Exchange is itself very unhappy about this. In its excellent quarterly review on the quality of markets, it admitted that spreads have risen by 50 per cent since Big Bang, a fact that was 'disappointing'.

Outside the City politicians still peddle the notion of popular capitalism, and one senses that the programmes of privatization have really only just begun. So omnivorous has been the encroachment of the state over the past century that it will take another decade for large and cumbersome enterprises to be parcelled out, and the process will inevitably be slowed down or halted if there should be a change of government.

So Big Bang, along with the sweeping technological changes, the new regime of regulation and investor protection and the wide variety of investment products and services, has not made a radical difference to the way capital is raised and the economy is run. Thatcher's revolution has had its limits. It has curbed the excesses of union power and the welfare state. But, despite privatization, it has done little to curb monopolies like British Gas, nor has it truly spread share ownership. Investment power still lies with the great institutions, and although the number of private shareholders has risen from five million to nine million, over half of them hold only one stock. Although informal share clubs like the one at the baked bean factory mentioned earlier still exist, there has been no great rush by the British public to buy equities or bonds. Mr and Mrs Average still prefer the betting shop or bingo parlour. There has been no proliferation of United States-style share shops in the towns and cities of Britain – and some of the most-publicized ventures have shut down.

The odds are stacked against individual ownership of shares. Privatization has encouraged quick gains by stagging, and not by long term ownership. Some believe, of course, that even if the opportunities for individual share ownership were better, the chances of most people using the stock markets would be low. At a *Financial Times* conference, Peter Hutton, a director of *MORI*, the research and opinion poll agency, argued that at least half the public were excluded because they had no cash. He said:

'In Britain, shareholding is still a luxury. While most people have some savings, other things have a call on funds. First call will be the necessities of life – food, clothing and shelter. Next will come consumer luxuries – a washing machine, car, or meals out. After that, marriage and owning your own property and security through insurance policies. Starting a family will require a larger property and more life assurance. Only when these needs are met will individuals start to accumulate wealth, and this is most likely to go into a building society or deposit account. Only when this has reached a safe buffer level is the small investor likely to look around at other ways of investing money. Even then stocks and shares have to compete with other forms of investment, such as unit trusts, endowment policies, and national savings schemes which have attractions which shares do not possess.'

Hutton says that those who are left are likely to be split into stags traders, loyalists, patriots and dabblers. Even in the United States,where the firm of Merrill Lynch invented the share shop under the label 'the firm that brought Wall Street to Main Street', there has been a decline in individual share ownership. On both sides of the Atlantic, families now tend to hand over management of their savings to institutions, whether they be unit trusts, mutual funds, pensions funds, life assurance companies, or banks. You can hardly blame them. The promotional hype of financial products has now exceeded even that evolved by Unilever and Proctor and Gamble for marketing soap powder, and the knock on the door by the Man from the Pru has been replaced by the 60–second commercial in the middle of ITN's News at Ten.

Although regulations restrict the claims that can be made, the development of databases and information technology has meant that a precise and detailed analysis of competitive investment performance is always available. And, as Stanislas Yassukovich pointed out in his Patrick Hutber Memorial Lecture in 1988:

'Whereas the pitch was: "Give me your savings to manage – I performed better than my competitors during the past 12 months", in the United States the pitch is now: "I performed better than my competitors last week". As the period of measurement for comparative investment performance shortens, those responsible for managing collective investment schemes seek better methods of ensuring better short-term performance.'

There are a variety of techniques they can deploy, such as

the use of futures and options contracts discussed earlier. Another popular development has been program trading, which was widely blamed for the October 1987 crash. The way this works is that chartists use specially created software to flash attention on dealers' screens when a crucial market indicator has been reached.

Another development now spreading into Britain from the United States is indexing. This involves the buying and holding of equities in proportions designed to equal precisely the performance of selected indices of the stock market. In America the most common of these is the Standard and Poor's 500, a selection of mostly large stocks in blue chip companies. In Britain the FT 30 Share Index of top industrial companies is used for the same purpose. The attraction of indexation is that it allows fund managers to show that, by mirroring the market, their investments have performed at least as well as the market. Since over a five year period to 1988, two-thirds of all British equity fund managers failed to match the FT-SE index, this is a goal which would content most long-term investors.

But constructing an equity portfolio to track any given index is not as easy as it sounds. The obvious way of doing it is to invest in all the stocks in the index at the same weightings as the index, and then adjust the portfolio whenever it changes. This is known as full-replication – the Swiss-owned stockbrokers Phillips and Drew use it. But the constant adjustments that have to be made involve considerable cost, and such a scheme is expensive to administer. A number of computer programs have been generated which will achieve roughly the same result, however. Once purchased, these will allow fund managers to sleep soundly in their beds confident that they have not made major errors of judgement. This technique is called optimization, and creates a sample portfolio from a stock market index which bears the characteristics of the index itself. Developed by a number of academics at Berkeley University in California while they were investigating the components of risk in equity portfolios, the Barra program is used extensively by the Bankers Trust in the United States, and has been adapted for use with the FT-SE index in London by Barclays de Zoete Wedd, County Natwest, and the United Bank of Kuwait. It is estimated that an optimized portfolio will track an index accurately at a value as low as £500,000, and therefore is a considerable attraction to institutions and pension fund trustees. But, as Yassukovich said in his lecture, such techniques serve to drive the individual investor away from stock markets:

'The individual considers himself ill-equipped to cope with these complexities of the market, having neither the time nor the computer power nor the access to professional dealing facilities to cope on his own. He becomes resigned, therefore, to handing over whatever proportion of savings he feels capable of investing directly to the unit trust or mutual fund. He will, of course, be heavily influenced by the short-term comparative performance statistics made available to him. This competitive process has given birth to the ugly phrase "short-termism", but those who most complain about its consequences are themselves caught up in the competitive nature of investment management. It is now a common experience to hear the same company chairman who complains bitterly of volatility in his company's share price – and the lack of loyalty demonstrated by institutions when a predator is on the prowl – coolly remark that he recently changed his pension fund manager because of inadequate experience during the last quarter'.

Yassukovich believes that this is of concern because individuals lose out. He is right. One of the most secure ways of harnessing public support for the capitalist system is to ensure that the public owns the system directly. It was this very tradition that helped to keep capitalism alive during periods of great stress, particularly after the Great Depression and World War II. But if the public is dissuaded from share ownership because of the power of the institutions in the market, it will start to resent the fund groups. After all, faceless men in the City are no different from faceless men in Whitehall – and even less accountable.

The Labour Party has sought to control the power of huge investment institutions, and still nurses the hope that one day it may be able to force the funds into industries and regions it believes need capital support. It probably has very little support for policies which would strip pension funds of their taxation privileges unless they agree to trim foreign investment to about half its present level of about 15 per cent of total portfolios. But Labour has not forgotten that within five years of exchange controls being abolished, more than £50 billion of portfolio investment found its way into overseas stocks.

Labour would try to force the funds to invest in Britain through a national investment bank, which would supposedly operate independently of Whitehall and Government, even though it would be subsidized by the taxpayer, and charge lower interest rates for projects deemed to be 'in the national interest'.

A blueprint for just such a bank but with rather less politicized goals, has been drawn up by the National Economic Development Council, an organization whose meandering thought processes over the years have contributed little to the aspirations implied by its name. Yet the idea does have the backing of some powerful voices in the City, including the Bank of England and Sir John Baring, chairman of Baring Brothers and part-time chairman of the NEDC committee on finance for industry. A starting equity base of about £100m. would, so it is believed, enable it to gear up to lending of up to £2.5bn., far too modest a sum to achieve any of Labour's major ambitions.

Baring's committee suggests that if such a bank were to be established its financing of industrial projects, both large and small, should be separated from any role it might have to make specific investments at the Government's request. It would provide funds for companies, wishing to embark on innovative projects and those on a recovery path, and there is also the suggestion that it could finance infrastructure projects such as roads, rail electrification, and the development of East Coast ports.

One has to have more than usual confidence in politicians to imagine that such a national investment bank would have genuine independence, and the outlook under such an economic regime is starting to look depressingly familiar.

But if Labour's way is to be avoided, the Conservatives will have to do a great deal more towards encouraging individual rather than institutional share ownership. One step that needs to be taken in future privatizations is to make sure that issues are pitched at only a shade below the market price, or, if it is considered sensible to offer giant state enterprises at a discount, to impose conditions which ensure that those who buy hold on to their shares for at least three years. This is a condition imposed in the sale of council houses at discounted rates, and there is no reason why it should not be applied in privatization. It would at least avoid the encouragement to 'stag' (to take a quick profit rather than a long-term view).

The government should also allow the public to take a much greater slice of future privatizations, rather than reserving such a large share for the institutions. The second course is much tidier, but it does leave most small investors with the feeling that they are there only to pick up the crumbs from under the table. When the number of shares allocated to members of the public is derisory – as was the case in the flotations of British Airways and the British Airports Authority – interest will not be sustained, and the public will become disaffected.

At no time was this sentiment expressed so vocally – on both sides of the Atlantic – as after the October crash of 1987. As the Brady Report into the crash indicated, a significant part of the selling pressure in New York resulted from the activity of five major institutions, all using computerized program-trading schemes. The public was actually a net buyer of shares at the time. Wall Street, in effect, told Main Street that they were in a mug's game.

Stanislas Yassukovich argues passionately that greater stability and greater protection can be found only through a shareholder register more balanced between individuals and institutions. To achieve this he suggests tax incentives for private shareholders.

At the end of the 1980s, the government was, of course, moving in the other direction – reducing the fiscal support for private home ownership in order to cut taxation to give individuals as much freedom of choice as possible with their disposable income. This policy, however, will rebound – for the more disposable income families have, the more they will develop the British propensity to import – whether it be foreign cars, holidays, hi-fi equipment or new German kitchens and bathrooms. So why not fiscal incentive for individual shareholdings to equate with tax relief for home ownership? At a time when the government plans to finance a major railway link with the Channel Tunnel and other schemes privately, as well as privatizing water, electricity, railways, steel and coal, this could start to redress the balance against the institutions. But it is unrealistic to expect that it would work unless accompanied by two other necessary developments.

The first is a major programme of education and public relations by the City to improve its image. The City has only itself to blame for the misconception in many people's minds that it is nothing much more than an up-market betting shop frequented by overpaid and spoilt young men and women. Television has done little to help. Despite the arrival of John Birt as news chief at the BBC 'with a mission to explain', the corporation's news bulletins nearly always illustrate important financial stories with pictures of dealers staring at screens and yelling at each other down the telephone. Explanation is minimal, and where it exists is often superficial. If the City is to get the message across to people, it must start to work collectively as well as competitively. Ever since Big Bang the forces of rivalry have been far greater than any spirit of enthusiasm for the common good; indeed such sentiment seems strangely absent from the Square Mile, almost as if no one really cared what the rest of Britain thought. Yet, to quote Yassukovich again:

'The City must spend more time talking to the rest of the world rather than to itself. We are too inward looking, and too inbred, if you like. We have got to bring Throgmorton Street to the High Street. If you travel around the United States, in almost every regional news programme, there are at least two or three daily stock market reports. Schools have investment clubs. Wall Street goes out and talks to them and to women's groups. Have you heard of a London stockbroker addressing a Women's Institute meeting. I am sure it has happened, but I must say I have never heard of it.'

To me, that says it all.

Secondly, the investing public must feel involved with the enterprises in which it holds shares. One small step in this direction has been the introduction by some boards of directors of shareholders' perks. One of the most enlightened companies in this regard is Sketchley. It offers those who have more than 300 shares a 25 per cent discount on dry cleaning. The company benefits, and the shareholders benefit. Three privately-owned railways pay no dividends on their shares, but provide shareholders with free tickets; in this case the shares are effectively enthusiasts' contributions. Trusthouse Forte has a scheme for those holding over 500 shares which effectively entitles them to a ten per cent discount on hotel bills and meals at Little Chef restaurants. Trafalgar House has a similar scheme for package holidays and voyages on the QE2. On a different tack, Rank Hovis McDougall gives all shareholders who attend the annual general meeting a bag of groceries to take home with them. The opportunities are endless, and a full list of the possible perks from shares is available in a book *Perks from Shares* published by chartered accountants Blackstone Franks.

Of course these schemes are very worthwhile and could and should be developed, but it will take more than some free perks to draw the public into full involvement with the stock markets. An intelligent approach is now being taken by some of the more enlightened people in the Labour Party, led by Bryan Gould. Gould canvasses the idea of employee share ownership plans, whereby employees could benefit from capital growth of their companies. It is not a particularly new idea: what is important is that it is a senior Labour figure who is advocating it. The Conservatives have been very slow to extend social ownership. Certainly much more radical change is needed than could be achieved by more privatization and public relations.

Greater public involvement will only come about when more private capital is raised at local level for local purposes. In the United States it is normal to raise funds for school extras – such as a swimming pool – from bond issues. There is no reason why proliferating public facilities such as leisure centres should not be financed in such a way.

At present the Thatcherite trend is for public services to be put out to contract – which does not necessarily improve them. The bureaucracy and inefficiency of local authorities is merely replaced by the greed of the company with the contract. Corners are cut and profits are maximized. This has become evident in the privatization of services as varied as local buses and school cleaning. For example, the streets used to be cleaned in my village, unsatisfactorily but reasonably frequently, by council employees. Now the budget allows a private contractor to do the work once a year. But if those of us in the village so minded could buy shares in a company which purchased cleaning equipment and employed an operative to serve the area, at the same time obtaining a reduction in rates, we would probably do so. We would also be likely to finance other local or regional enterprises, and take an interest in their prosperity. Medium-sized companies, too small, perhaps, for a listing on the International Stock Exchange, might join a local exchange, where their shares could be traded. Unfortunately the City elitists have shown no interest in this kind of development, principally, one suspects, because the income derived would be too small to meet their extravagant overheads. This has meant that local industry has been financed principally by the trading banks, which have done a reasonable job, although it has not accelerated the spread of share ownership in the way Britain needs so badly today.

The London Stock Exchange has either failed to see the significance of these developments, or perhaps has been too busy pursuing its international ambitions. It is to its credit that so much business has been attracted to London, but the very electronic systems introduced to make this possible have, ironically, left Throgmorton Street even more uncertain about its role.

Its trading floor is now longer needed now that securities markets have moved on screen. Its regulatory role has been taken over by the Securities Association and the Securities and Investment Board. With TAURUS, settlement will be wholesaled through big securities houses and the banks. It faces competition on information services.

Staff numbers have been cut in the past few years by one-third to just over 2,000, and it is hard to believe that all those remaining are usefully employed. What is left for them to do?

As Richard Waters argued in March 1991 in the *Financial Times*: 'Like peeling an onion, it would be possible to strip away all the layers and leave nothing in the centre'.

The council of the LSE has recently been reconstituted and reduced in size, but with a broader spread of members so that industry and the institutional investors are represented.

This group now has the task to ensure that the organization remains a force in the markets.

How can this be achieved? Not, I suggest, by trying to carry out functions that are better achieved out in the market itself. SEAQ has become a success, and can be developed and improved upon so that it becomes the global trading standard. At the other end of the spectrum a more limited version of SEAQ covering the major UK shares could be built for access from High Street banks: the LSE needs to show that it can spread its tentacles to the grass roots. Its police force watching for dubious trades has been effective, and the LSE should try to regain more of a supervisory role.

It should lead with advice and assistance to those in Eastern Europe and the Soviet Union trying to set up equity and bond markets, rather than leave this to international accountancy firms with high fees. And above all, it should seek to remain an important cog in the international wheel of stock markets.

For their part the banks and securities houses should start taking steps to widen share ownership, rather than trying to dump collective securities like unit trusts on an unreceptive public. I am not alone in this view. When John Major was Chancellor of the Exchequer, he challenged stockbrokers to lower costs and make the equity market more accessible to the small investor. He criticized the LSE for abandoning its proposed second-tier stockmarket, which could have provided better buying and selling prices for small investors. And his Treasury paper urged brokers to build on the achievements of privatization to create a mass retail business.

Major was right, and clearly has a keener sense of what the British public need than the City of London. Within a few months of becoming Prime Minister he has made it clear that he wants future privatization issues to be sold through High Street banks and building societies 'in a cheap and accessible way'. The plan to move sales of the final privatization of the remainder of British Telecom from the City to the High Street is a good one. Share ownership schemes for employees are to be extended, with especially favourable tax treatment for those companies that extend them to all their workers, not just the senior management. Additionally companies that give their workers profit sharing through shares

may do so tax free up to quite high limits. And more emphasis is to be put on personal equity plans – whereby no tax
is paid on dividends and capital gains if the investment is
held in place for five years. In 1991 it was impossible to
invest £9,000 a year in such schemes, without being forced
to pay tax.

Most of these schemes will be devised by arrangements
which bypass those in the City who have taken out so much,
and given so little.

Index

accountancy
  Association of Chartered
    Accountants 153
  fees 98
  international 22
acquisitions *see* takeovers
Acquisitions Monthly 114, 144
advertising
  Barlow Clowes affair 160
  costs 94
  legal requirements for 157–8
  legal restrictions on 69–70
  of bond issues 22
  of share auctions 14
  or share issues 35, 92, 103
  of share prices 28
Alfred Herbert 96
*Alliance and Leicester Building
  Society* 21
Allied Lyons 122–3, 127
American Express 32
analysts 5, 135–7
Ariel 5
Artom, Guido 141
asset-stripping 107

Baker, Kenneth 101
Bank of England 29, 32, 83, 108,
  160, 162
Banque Bruxelles Lambert SA 22
Banque Indosuez 22
Barclays Bank plc 32, 49, 50, 113,
  139, 155
Barclays De Zoete Wedd see BZW
Barclayshare 62, 80, 139
Baring Brothers and Co. Ltd 71,
  170
Barlow Clowes affair 159–63
Bass 97
bear market 12, 27

Bellini, James 64
Berrill, Sir Kenneth 152–5
'best execution' rule 154
beta stocks *see* stocks
Bevan 32, 123, 149
Big Bang 3, 18, 24–34, 36, 37, 98,
  165, 166, 172
Bishopsgate PEP unit trust 68
'Black Monday' 34–7, 107, 160
blue-chip stocks *see* stocks
Blunt, Sir John 11–12
Boardman, Lord 161
Boesky, Ivan F 7, 106, 148, 151
Bokros, Lajos 57
Bond, Alan 107
bond finance 21
bond issues 79
bonds
  Eurobonds 20–3, 95, 99
  interest-bearing *see* gilt-edged
    securities
  zero-coupon 21
Borrie, Sir Gordon 156
Bowater, Corporation 71
breweries 1, 2
British Airports Authority 171
British Airways 88, 103, 137, 138,
  171
British Gas 11, 59, 87–8, 101,
  103, 166
British Leyland 96
British Petroleum 3, 34, 35, 43,
  51, 76, 81
British Sky Broadcasting 7, 107
British Steel 103
British Telecom 11, 13, 31, 59, 77,
  88, 101, 102, 103, 138
Britoil 93
Brokerline 139

brokers
  Big Bang 3, 18, 24–34, 36, 37,
    98, 165, 166, 172
  commission 5, 8, 24, 25, 26–7,
    28, 62, 69, 155–6
  licensing of 8
  pitches 14–15
  research 5, 28
  small/private investors 5, 22, 33,
    36, 37, 58–65, 157, 167, 170
bull market 27, 79, 85, 120
BZW 1, 6, 32, 43, 115, 139, 145,
  168

Cabot, Sebastian 9
Cadman, Roger 86
Capel Court 15–16
Capital Gains Tax 74
Capital Transfer Tax 90
capitalism 6, 166
Cazenove and Co. 33
CBI Wider Share Ownership
  Council 58, 59
Central Share Register 80
Channel Tunnel 172
Chase Manhattan 86
Chase Securities 145
Chicago Board Options
  Exchange 82
Chinese Walls 158–9
Citicorp 32, 36, 113
City of London 3, 17–20
City Takeover Code 108
City Takeover Panel 109
Clowes, Peter 161
commercial law 22
'commercial paper' 23–4
commission see brokers
communications costs 18
Computer Assisted Trading
  Systems (CATS) 47
Consumer Federation of America
  (CFA) 149
Cornfeld, Bernie 72
Corporation of London 18
Corporation Tax 99

Daiwa 50
Datsun UK 51

DAX (Deutscher Aktienindex) 55
dealers see brokers
debt financing 96
deregulation 97, 141–63
Deutschebank 32
dividends 79, 103
Dobson Park 102
Dow Chemical 71
Dow Jones 129
Dow Jones Industrial Average 34
Drucker, Peter 101
'dual-dealing system' 5, 6
Dunlop 96

East India Company 9, 53
Elders-IXL 122–3, 127
electronic trading 1–6, 24–34 see
  also Big Bang
Elliott, John 122–3
employee share ownership 85–8
Employee Share Ownership Plans
  (ESOPS) 86–7
equities
  market 20, 55
  trading 30–1
Ernst, Dr Gernot 54
ethical trusts 66–7
Eurobond market 20–3, 95, 99
European Currency Unit
  (ECU) 21, 22, 95
European Investment Bank 99

FAZ index 55
Federation of German Stock
  Exchanges 54
Figlewski, Stephen 82
Financial Adviser 68
financial advisers 138–40
Financial Intermediaries,
  Managers and Brokers
  Regulatory Association
  (FIMBRA) 153, 159, 160
Financial Services Act 151–2, 157,
  161
Financial Times All-Share
  Index 68
fixed commissions 5, 24, 26–7, 28
fixed-interest securities 59, 63
Ford 24

foreign exchange 17–18, 22
fraud *see* insider trading
fund managers 1, 5, 33, 63, 72, 84
'fund of funds' 72–5
futures
   Futures Brokers and Dealers,
     Association of (AFBD) 153
   gilt-edged securities 14, 32, 34,
     65, 155, 161
   'hedging' 83
   junk bonds 121–2, 128
   LIFFE 83

Galbraith, John Kenneth 35
General Motors 24
gilt-edged securities 14, 32, 34, 65,
   155, 161
Goldman Sachs 23, 124
Goodison, Sir Nicholas 17, 25, 26,
   29, 30, 31
Gorbachev, Mikhail 59
government debt *see* National
   Debt
Gower, Jim 151–2
Gower Report 151–2
'Great Crash' 1929 34–5, 120,
   148
GT Management
Guinness 7, 90, 144, 147
Guinness affair 7, 147, 162

Halifax building society 74
Hapern, Sir Ralph 116
Hambros Investment
   Management 71
Hanson, Lord 114–15
Hanson Trust 81, 97, 114–15,
   123–6
Harrington, Kathryn Rudie 126–7
Healey, Denis 19
'hedging' 83
Heller, Robert 17
Heron International Finance
   NV 22
Hill Samuel 71
history of the stockmarket 7–16
Hoare Govett 36, 43, 75
Hodgson, Godfrey 72
Holmes à Court, Robert 105, 117

Honda 51
House of Novura 7
Hudson, George 13

IBM 24, 45, 71
ICI 25, 34, 51, 76, 77, 81, 134
inflation 5, 27, 99
information technology 1, 18,
   24–5, 129–35
Inland Revenue 79
insider information 33, 141–63
insider trading 8, 141–63
interest rates 23, 99, 112
international accountancy 22
International Bank for
   Reconstruction and
   Development 22
international bonds *see* Eurobonds
International Securities Regulatory
   Organization (ISRO) 30–1
International Stock
   Exchange 79–80
investment banking 22
Investment Management
   Regulatory Organization
   (IMRO) 153
investment trusts 66, 69–70
investor relations 133–5
investors
   confidence 143
   dealing rates 157
   employee 85–8
   Financial Services Act, impact
     of 153
   institutional 2, 5, 22, 23, 24, 33,
     34, 59, 64, 66, 101, 157, 170
   perks 172–3
   small/private 5, 22, 33, 36, 37,
     58–65, 157, 167, 170
Investors Overseas Services 73
Isotron 92, 93

J Henry Schroder Wagg and
   Co. 71–2, 93
jobbers 3–4, 5
J P Morgan 50
junk bonds 121–2, 128

Klaus, Vaclav 52

'know your customer' rule 154
Kohl, Helmut 52
Kurs Information Services System
    (KISS) 55

Labour Party 19, 66, 169, 173
Lazard Securities 71
Legal and General 37
Li, Ronald 8
Life Assurance and Unit Trust
    Regulatory Organization
    (LAUTRO) 153, 156
life assurance companies 1, 2,
    33–4, 63, 65–8, 98
London International Financial
    Futures Exchange (LIFFE) 83
Lloyds Bank 51, 77, 155
Lloyds Merchant Bank Ltd 22
loan capital 98, 99
loan stock 98
London Business School 18
London Stock Exchange *see* stock
    exchanges
Lyons, Sir Jack 147

Macmillan, Harold 101
mailshots *see* advertising
Major, John 175
managed funds 70–72, 74
market-makers 2, 6, 35, 39, 40,
    41, 42, 44, 94, 105, 124, 125,
    129, 145
market-rigging 8, 157–9
Marx, Karl 85
Maxwell, Robert 113
McKinsey 108
Mecca group 145–6
merchant banks 5, 31
Mercury 32
mergers 110–11
Merrill Lynch 23, 32, 57, 134,
    148, 167
Mesler, Donald 81
Midland Bank 51, 155
Milken, Michael 8
Money Management 68
Monopolies Commission 26, 111,
    116, 127

*Montague Investment
    Management* 69, 71
Morgan Grenfell 45
Morgan, J Pierpont 110
Muscovy Company 8–9, 53
mutual funds 63, 149

National Association of Securities
    Dealers Automated
    Quotation System
    (NASDAQ) 6, 39–42, 150
National Association of Security
    Dealers 41
National Debt 11, 14
National Economic Development
    Council 170
NatWest Bank, 139, 155
NEC 50
net asset value 70
New York Stock Exchange *see*
    stock exchanges
Nikko 50
Nissan 48, 51
*N M Rothschild Asset
    Management Ltd* 72
Nomura 32, 47–51
Norrington, Humphrey 49
Northumbrian Water 87
Norwich Union 155

Office of Fair Trading 5, 25–6,
    156
Old Bailey 7
options 81–2, 168
over-gearing 96
over-subscription 96

Packer, Kerry 106, 107
PA Consulting Group 86
Page, Bruce 72
Parnes, Anthony 147
pension funds 2, 5, 33, 63, 64–5,
    98
Personal Equity Plan (PEP)
    schemes 155
Phillips and Drew 37, 71, 93, 168
portfolio management 63
Price Information Project Europe
    (PIPE) 54

preference shares 111
Pre-emption Group 98
price-setting *see* shares
privatization 11, 35, 37, 59, 63,
    87–8, 101–4, 157, 166, 172
prospectuses 91–2, 157
*Prudential Assurance
    Company* 25, 37
public relations, of City of
    London 164

Radcliffe, Lord 19
Rank Organization 102
Raw, Charles 72
Really Useful Group 93
regulation 141–63 *see also* self-
    regulation of the Stock
    Exchange
research *see* brokers research
'restrictive practices' 26
Reuters 129–30
Reuter Money Line service 40
rights issues 79, 96, 97–8, 121
*Robert Fleming Investment
    Management Ltd* 71
Ronson, Gerald 22, 147
Rooke, Sir Denis 101
Royal National Lifeboat
    Institution 71

salespeople 1–2, 6
Sampson, Anthony 53
satellite television 7
Saunders, Ernest 147
Savage, John 75
Save and Prosper Group 66
savings funds 5
Savory Milln 37
SCM Corporation 123–6
Scott, W R 10
Scottish Life Assurance 37
securities
    business 29
    houses 6, 31, 47, 140, 157
Securities Administrators
    Association 149
Securities and Exchange
    Commission (SEC) 19,
    147–52, 162

Securities and Investment Board
    (SIB) 19, 152, 153, 154, 157,
    161, 162, 174
Securities Association, The
    (TSA) 153
Securities Investor Protection
    Corporation 42
Security Pacific Alliance 36
Seelig, Roger 147
self-regulation 29–30, 108, 147,
    148, 153–4
Sepon Ltd 79
S G Warburg and Co. 32
shareholders *see* investors
Sharelink 140
shares
    certificates 75–80
    fund of funds 72–5
    hyping 157
    institutional investors 2, 5, 22,
        23, 24, 33, 34, 59, 64, 66,
        101, 157, 170
    investment trusts 66, 69–70
    life assurance companies 1, 2,
        33–4, 63, 65–8, 98
    managed funds 70–2, 74
    ordinary 27
    pension funds 2, 5, 33, 63,
        64–5, 98
    preference 111
    price-setting 2, 87, 93–4, 96–7,
        105
    purchase 2
    purchase/sales sliding scale 27
    rights issue 79, 96, 97–8, 121
    selling 29
    stagging 13, 93, 102, 171
Shell 51
short-termism 33–4, 169
Sinclair Research 112
Sinclair, Sir Clive 112
Smith, Andrew Hugh 60
Sony 50
South Sea Company 11–12
speculation *see* futures
stagging 13, 93, 102, 171
stamp duty 25, 27, 69, 79
Stapf, Scott 141

Stock Exchange Automated
    Quotations Systems
    (SEAQ) 42–6, 56, 145, 175
Stock Exchange Council 25, 26
Stock Exchange Daily Official
    List 10
Stockbrokers *see* brokers
Stock Exchange examinations 30
stock exchanges
    Eastern European 56–7
    London 1, 3, 4, 5, 6, 7, 14–16,
        54
    New York 6, 37–40, 54, 120
    regional 14
    Tokyo 6, 47–51, 54
stockmarket crashes *see* 'Black
    Monday' *and* 'Great Crash
    1929'
stocks
    alpha, beta and gamma 43
    blue-chip 66, 168
    convertible 98
    loan 98
    'recovery' 66
Swiss Banking Corporation 32,
    37, 56
Sumitomo Chemical Company 22

takeovers
    asset-stripping 107
    City Takeover Code 108
    City Takeover Panel 109
    insider dealing 8, 141–63
    junk bonds 121–2, 128
    Monopolies Commission 26,
        111, 116, 127
    Office of Fair Trading 5, 25–6,
        156
    preference shares 111
takeover bids 64
Talisman system 77–9, 80
taxation 5, 14, 21, 67, 87, 95, 169
Thatcher Government 26, 59, 101,
    111
Thatcher, Margaret 24, 57, 166

Third World loans 23
Thompson, Sir Peter 58, 59
Thorn EMI 113
Thurow, Lester 52
Timex 113
Tokyo Stock Exchange *see* stock
    exchanges
TOPIC information service 43
Toyota 50, 51
Trade and Industry, Department
    of 74, 110, 144, 148, 150,
        151, 152, 156, 159–60
Transfer and Automated
    Registration of Uncertified
    Stock (TAURUS) 80, 174

UBS 71
underwriters 21, 35, 92–3
Unilever 34, 51
Union de Banque Suisse 37, 56
unit trusts 2, 34, 61, 63, 66–8, 96,
    144
Unlisted Securities Market
    (USM) 99–100
US Securities and Exchange
    Commission (SEC) 73, 82,
        147–52

VAT 25, 81

Wall Street 2, 34, 37–40, 106
Walpole, Sir Robert 12
*Warburg Investment
    Management* 72
Wedd, Durlacher & Mordaunt 32
Weinberg, Sir Mark 156
Whitbread 71
Wilson, Lord 19
World Bank 99

Yamaichi 50
Yassukovich, Stavislas 1, 167,
    169, 171, 172
Young and Rubicam 103